# Developing Good Movement Skills

## for

# 4–11 year olds

**Alan Pearson**
**and David Hawkins**


**A & C Black ● London**

## Metric to Imperial conversions

| | | |
|---|---|---|
| 1 centimetre (cm) | = | 0.394 in |
| 1 metre (m) | = | 1.094 yd |
| 1 kilometre (km) | = | 1093.6 yd |
| 1 kilogram (kg) | = | 2.205 lb |

First published 2005 by A&C Black Publishers Ltd
37 Soho Square, London WID 3OZ
www.acblack.com

Copyright © 2005 by SAQ Internationl Ltd

ISBN 0 71367041X

A CIP catalogue record for this book is available from the British Library.

A&C Black uses paper produced with elemental chlorinefree pulp, harvested from managed sustainable forests.

## Acknowledgements

Cover photograph courtesy of Ariel Skelley/Corbis, all other photographs courtesy of SAQ International; illustrations courtesy of Angus Nicol.

Typeset in Photina
Printed any bound in Great Britain
by Biddles Ltd, King's Lynn

# Contents

# Acknowledgements

It has taken three years for the SAQ Junior Programme to be accepted as a fundamental tool to assist in the development of young children. In that time it has been my good fortune to work with many inspiring and dedicated parents, teachers and coaches nationwide. To all of you who have embraced the programme and believed in its potential to bring about real change in children, I extend my heartfelt thanks.

This continuing journey would not have been possible without the support of a team of very special people. To Alan, thanks for your vision and inspiration, as without you none of this would be possible. To Sarah, Silvana, Angus, Brian, Marc, Mike, Becky, and Danny at SAQ International, a huge thank you for your support, advice, and encouragement.

A special mention must be made of a number of superb professionals who have believed in and embraced our work; Geoff Sheldon, Alan Duff, Kim Hazeldine and Sue Odgers, Vanessa Forster, Leigh Marshall, Peter Tolvey and Jenny Smith.

Special thanks go also to the staff and pupils at Danemill Primary School, Enderby in Leicestershire and the staff and pupils at St Peter and St Paul Primary School, Syston in Leicestershire. To Becky, Lucy, Martha, Rosie, Taylor, James, Matt and Ryan for featuring in the wonderful photographs and to Steve Gilbert for the fantastic graphics.

Finally my thanks to my family, Simone and Theresa who continue to inspire me every single day and my dear cousin Sally, a constant in my life.

**David Hawkins**
January 2005

I would like to thank all those hundreds of teachers that I have spent time with for their support and feedback on our SAQ Schools Programmes. Their encouragement and desire to improve physical performance for young children with the implementation of our SAQ Programme for Juniors has inspired both myself and David to write this book. I would also like to thank all the staff at SAQ International and particularly my wife, Silvana, for their on-going support.

**Alan Pearson**
January 2005

# Forewords

Our school sport partnership has long believed in promoting the development of a 'fundamental skills' approach to teaching PE and sport in schools. We have encouraged teachers and coaches to focus on helping young people to become all-round performers, with a broad range of skills, knowledge and understanding, which will stay with them for the rest of their lives.

SAQ alongside our own staff and the Durham University On-Fitness team, has played an integral part in this development by continuously providing expert training and resources over the past three years.

SAQ deserve a great deal of credit for promoting an innovative approach and philosophy, which can have a huge impact on teaching and learning in schools. They have a strong commitment to developing sports performance in young people, with a philosophy of delivering through fun, exciting, simple yet challenging activities. SAQ Junior is an invaluable tool for every primary link teacher in helping them to develop high quality PE and sport within their school.

**Geoff Sheldon, PDM**
**District of Easington SSCo Partnership**

I have worked with professional footballers for many years, and I have always been interested in researching and implementing programmes and techniques that are beneficial to the rehabilitation, training and conditioning of footballers. As a parent with young children who enjoy participating in physical activity at school, I am constantly aware of the most successful and innovative programmes available.

I was introduced to the SAQ training programme over six years ago and was immediately impressed. I have used the programme successfully with all levels of players from senior international stars to young academy players. I have also used the programme with my children who have responded positively to the different techniques and drills. It is fantastic that young children can perform the same drills and skills within the SAQ programme that are performed by elite athletes and stars in a number of sports.

I highly recommend SAQ Junior as a must for all those working with young children. It is easy to read, easy to implement and fun.

**John Green, BSc HONS, MCSP, SRP**
**Head Physiotherapist, West Ham United FC**

In my view, SAQ programmes complement the PE curriculum and school sport, and provide valuable and essential co-ordination and movement experiences for age groups from Foundation Stage to Key Stage 4. SAQ training activities are providing new, enjoyable, achievable and challenging activities for children and their teachers.

The programme in County Durham has been further adapted by the Educational Psychology Service as part of their intervention programme to support children of all ages with identified movement and co-ordination problems. As a result the SAQ programme in County Durham has been described by a primary headteacher as 'the best innovation I have experienced throughout my career available to all children in all schools.'

**Alan Duff**
**Advisory teacher for Physical Education,**
**Durham LEA**

# Introduction

During recent times our society has changed dramatically and with it the way in which children occupy their time. Who would have thought that children would walk around making phone calls on mobile phones via satellite transmitters and spend hours accessing information via the internet on state-of-the-art portable computers? Television has become the focal point of many families' lives, providing images instantly from around the world. This influence in particular has had an enormous effect on the way in which children conduct their everyday lives. Many images seen by children have not been positive in terms of healthy lifestyle, with advertising and marketing constantly bombarding them with the temptations of, for example, food products not considered healthy by nutritionists.

This 'progress' has been at the expense of something that used to be taken for granted – physical activity. Currently the United Kingdom is second to America in having the most obese population in the world. The cost in the future to the nation's health will be catastrophic if effective strategies are not developed to bring about a change. Some suggest it will be similar to a 'pile-up on the motorway of health', costing the government billions of taxpayers' money.

Not so long ago our experiences were different. There was not just an educational, but a societal focus on allowing children to play and exercise, at school, in the streets, and in parks. It was a common sight to see children playing in the street, running, skipping, dodging, and playing hopscotch and other games. In schools, playground activities were commonplace, as was walking to school. Now children are picked up and dropped off at school by car and some competitive games are discouraged due to health and safety concerns. In many primary schools time allocated to Physical Education (PE), dance, movement and drama no longer has equal standing with the more academic subjects.

With participation levels in many of our sports and activities also dropping as many children and families prefer other, less physical activities, and poor performances of UK athletes in many of the world's elite sports hitting the headlines, movement experiences and activity levels of today's children have become major issues. This has prompted the present government to look to the future with a strategy called Game Plan (DCMS, www.culture.gov.uk).

Another concern is that 'adolescent girls are less likely than their male counterparts to participate in PE and sport' particularly between the ages of 16 and 24 years (British Heart Foundation). This trend is not assisted by an imbalance in the reporting of sport by the media. You only have to look at the newspapers to discover that the majority of reports are on male sports and in the event of a female being featured it is often because of looks and physical shape rather than actual performance. Participation by girls in physical education and the appropriateness of curriculum activities have also become current issues (Girls in Sport, Nike/Youth Sport Trust Project).

Even though there is now a government initiative to ensure all schools provide two hours of PE a week as an entitlement, and recent research by the QCA, PE project 2000, (Qualification and Curriculum Authority) actually points to the fact that children who are involved in physical activity and sport can attain higher academic standards, some schools no longer have much space or school fields and a focus on numeracy and literacy dominates curriculum time, because of the drive to improve academic standards.

Many of our primary school teachers do not have a background in sport and have received only a small number of hours' training to teach physical education. This has lead to a lack of confidence when delivering PE lessons. Primary teachers have a crucial role in developing future athletes. Fortunately, support structures are now being put in place successfully through the School Sport Co-ordinators programme (overseen by the Youth Sport Trust).

By coincidence recent independent research conducted by the Leeds Metropolitan University (Bailey and Morley 2003) in conjunction with SAQ International indicated that the SAQ Schools Programme had a positive impact not only on pupils but also on the staff in terms of self-esteem and self-confidence. Staff felt confident and empowered by the SAQ Training Programme and appreciated the potential of its inclusion in everyday teaching.

Another feature becoming more apparent is the increasing identification of children in numbers who have specific learning difficulties: dyslexia, dyspraxia and Attention Deficit Hyperactivity Disorder (ADHD) (Portwood 2003). Research indicates that there is a link between such problems and deficits in motor skills and a major factor in tackling these problems is to provide structured and sequential movement programmes at all stages of a child's development.

It can thus be seen, that the provision for PE and sports participation is at present coming under scrutiny against a background of major concerns about children's participation in activity and the state of their general health.

## Fundamental movement development

Movement in children develops from generic movement patterns to increasingly specific and specialised actions (Bailey and Macfadyen 2000). Initially by exploring their environments and through trial and error children develop visual skills, posture/balance, co-ordination and a whole range of motor skills. At the same time awareness of speed and distance develops along with auditory and perceptual skills.

It is between the ages of 2 and 7 that children lay down the foundations needed to acquire and refine the basic skills of stability, locomotion and manipulation upon which later abilities such as sporting skills are built.

As well as experience of movement opportunities, changes in growth, i.e. size and proportion of the body, can have major effects upon the ways in which children perform physical skills. During childhood the head doubles in length, the trunk trebles, the arms quadruple and legs increase fivefold (NCF 1994) making children 'bottom heavy'.

This can affect performance of skills, with balance, dexterity, co-ordination and timing of actions all suffering. As children develop at different rates, this would suggest that a focus on the development of fundamental movement skills should continue throughout physical education and sports training experiences, thus maintaining a foundation for all skills learning.

Equally important is the timing and the order in which these skills are introduced. There has perhaps been a tendency when introducing activity specific programmes to focus immediately on the development of manipulation skills without due attention to those skills that should precede them, i.e. those listed under the headings of stability and locomotion.

As previously stated there is growing evidence that many children do not experience appropriate movement opportunities necessary for the development of basic movement abilities (Walkley et al. 1993).

It is vital that children experience the full range of the skills listed in Table 1 (Sugden and Talbot 1998).

## FUNDAMENTAL SKILLS

| Stability | Locomotion | Manipulation |
|---|---|---|
| Bending | Walking | Throwing |
| Stretching | Running | Catching |
| Twisting | Jumping | Kicking |
| Turning | Hopping | Trapping |
| Swinging | Skipping | Striking |
| Inverted supports | Galloping | Volleying |
| Body rolling | Sliding | Bouncing |
| Landing/Stopping | Leaping | Ball rolling |
| Dodging | Climbing | Punting |

Table 1. (Development PE for All Children David L Gallahue, F Cleland Donnelly)

## Specialised movement development

Having acquired a reasonable level of competence in the basics, children between 7 and 10 years of age – the 'skill hungry years' (Maunde 1996; Williams 1996) – seek out opportunities to increase therange and quality of their movement.

Now is the time for introducing greater structure, more explicit rules and more clearly defined roles. Motivation is rarely a problem, so the teacher/coach must capitalise upon the children's desire to improve or the result can be longterm under-performance and even disenchantment with physical activity. By developing the basic skills learned and practised during the early years, children are better able to perform more specialised, general activity/sports-specific movements. They do this by refining, combining and elaborating upon their fundamental movement skills.

Engaging children in vigorous, exhilarating and fun learning experiences must be the goal of every playtime, physical education lesson and sports training lesson. These sessions will of course be multiskilled and should involve co-ordination, movement, decision-making and body awareness.

The above observations indicate the importance of parents, teachers/coaches and educators utilising every possible means to allow children the opportunities to enjoy and participate successfully in physical activity. One of the most effective and successful, stimulating and easy-to-use method is SAQ TRAINING.

## What is SAQ Training?

## Speed

Children enjoy the sensation of running fast. If this ability is to be developed a crucial part of the child's development is the ability to cover ground efficiently and economically over the first few metres and then open the stride length and increase stride frequency to cover a longer distance. Speed means the maximum velocity a child can achieve and maintain usually over a short distance. In the mechanics section of the Junior Continuum (see page 61) there is a great deal of focus on performing correct running mechanics. This will improve running technique which in turn will be integrated into all aspects of the child's physical activity. The best runners spend little time in contact with the ground.

# Agility

Agility is the ability to change direction without the loss of balance, co-ordination, strength, speed and body control. Therefore to train agility all these areas need to be practised. Agility should not be taken for granted and can be taught to children so that they can become more efficient. Good agility also helps prevent niggling injuries by teaching the muscles how to 'fire' properly and control minute shifts in ankle, knee, hip, back, shoulder and neck joints for optimum body alignment. Another very important benefit of agility training with children is that it is long lasting. A younger person is more responsive to programming of muscle memories and will retain and repeat movements automatically.

## THE FOUR STAGES OF AGILITY

There are four stages to developing agility:

1. Balance

2. Co-ordination

3. Programmed agility

4. Random agility

Although these stages are subtle in difference and often overlap, understanding each stage helps to simplify the teaching and learning process (Smyth).

Balance is the foundation of athleticism. Here the ability to stand, walk and stop while focusing on the centre of gravity, good posture and foot placement can be taught and the feeling of balance retained relatively quickly. Examples include: standing on one leg, standing on a balance beam, walking on a balance beam, standing on an agility disc, walking backwards with your eyes closed and jumping on a mini-trampoline and then freezing. It does not take too long to train balance. It requires only a couple of minutes, two or three times a week.

Co-ordination is the goal of mastering simple skills under more difficult stresses. 'It is an activity that involves two or more processes' (Portwood 2003). Co-ordination work is often slow and methodical with an emphasis on correct biomechanics during athletically demanding movements. Training co-ordination can be completed by breaking a skill down into sections then gradually bringing them together again. Co-ordination activities include footwork drills, circuit runs, 'mirror' movements, rhythmic and sequential activities such as bouncing a ball, and jumping. More difficult examples are walking through a ladder while playing catch or performing 'hop, skip and jump'.

The third stage of agility training is called programmed agility. Before complex manipulation skills can be learned and many difficult sports movements mastered it is necessary to experience the patterns and sequences of movement, for example in learning to play a forehand in tennis it is beneficial to rehearse the 'ready' position sequence, racket back, step to the side, and swing the racket forward, sequence as a 'shadow' without a ball before a rally is experienced. When the child understands how to replicate the movement programme, they can then give their attention to the speed, flight and direction of the ball. Likewise in performing dodging movements in a game, it is far better to practise a series of different movement patterns in a circuit before having to focus on a whole number of other movement decisions, for example, where is the target, where are the opponents, when must one move and where are one's team-mates?

Programmed agility drills can be conducted at high speeds but must be learnt at low, controlled speeds. Examples are zigzag marker spot drills, shuttle runs and 'T' spot drills, all of which involve changing direction along a known standardised pattern. There is no spontaneity of movement involved in this process.

Once these types of drills are learnt and performed on a regular basis, times and performances will improve and advances in strength, explosion, flexibility and body control will be witnessed. This is true of children of any ability.

The final stage and most difficult to master, prepare for and perform is random agility. Here the child performs tasks with unknown patterns and unknown demands. Here the teacher/coach can incorporate visual and audible reactive skills so that the child has to make split-second decisions with movements based upon the various stimuli. The skill level is now becoming much closer to the 'chaos' experienced in actual game situations. Random agility can be trained by games such as tag, read-and-react ball drills and more specific training such as jumping and landing followed by an immediate unexpected movement demand from the teacher.

Agility training is challenging, fun and exciting. There exists the opportunity for tremendous variety ensuring that training does not become boring or laborious. Agility is not just for those with elite sporting abilities – try navigating through a busy shopping mall!

## Quickness

When a performer accelerates, a great deal of force has to be generated and transferred through the foot to the ground. This action is similar to that of rolling a towel up (the 'leg'), holding one end in your hand and flicking it out to achieve a cracking noise from the other end (the 'foot').

The act of acceleration takes the body from a static position to motion in a fraction of a second. Muscles actually lengthen and then shorten instantaneously – the process being an 'eccentric' followed by a 'concentric' contraction. This is known as the stretch shortening cycle action (SCC).

SAQ Training concentrates on improving the neuro-muscular system that impacts on this process, so that this initial movement – whether lateral, linear or vertical–is automatic, explosive and precise. The reaction time is the time it takes for the brain to receive and respond to a stimulus by sending a message to the muscle causing it to contract. This is what helps a child when playing a game to cut right – left – right again and then sprint down the sideline, or the goalkeeper to make a split-second reaction save. With ongoing SAQ Training, the neuro-muscular system is reprogrammed and restrictive mental blocks and thresholds are removed. Consequently messages from the brain have a clear path to the muscles, and result is an instinctively quicker child.

Quickness training begins with 'innervation' (isolated fast contractions of an individual joint). For example, repeating the same explosive movement over a short period of time, such as fast feet and line drills. These quick repetitive motions take the body through the 'gears' moving it in a co-ordinated manner to develop speed. Integrating quickness training throughout the year by using fast feet and reaction-type drills will result in the muscles having increased 'firing' rates. This means that children are capable of faster, more controlled acceleration. The goal is to ensure that your children explode over the first 1–3 metres. Imagine that the firing between the nervous system and the muscles are the gears in a car. The right timing, speed and smoothness of the gear change means the wheels and thus the car accelerate away efficiently, so that the wheels do not spin and the driver does not lose control.

This successful and effective training method can be taught to children through the SAQ Junior Programme.

## What is the SAQ Junior Programme?

Multidirectional footwork and body control, hand–eye co-ordination, agility, balance, running and jumping, together with a whole range of manipulation skills such as throwing and catching, will contribute greatly to developing fundamental movements and sports skills. These are the keys for children to access and enjoy the numerous physical education and sporting experiences available to them.

If these motor skills have been developed through early repetition they become engrained on the muscle memory and will serve the children for years to come. The brain stores this information and eventually the 'planning' of movements becomes instinctive and reflexive, described by Nicolson and Fawcett (1990) as the 'automatisation of skills'. This can and will bring untold benefits to all participants who continue to have active lifestyles.

The SAQ Junior Programme is a framework for the development of fundamental motor skills which compliments the national PE curriculum activity areas and national governing body teacher/coach sports coaching structures. The programme is based on sound physiological research and its practical application with children (to date in over 500 UK schools), adults, and amateur and elite athletes. Much experience has also been gained from its implementation in the health and fitness industry.

The SAQ Junior Programme resource offers unique programmes that provide simple, well-structured and easy-to-understand activities for children of all abilities and aspirations. It allows parents, teachers/coaches to guarantee a major impact when developing the ability of children to move in a co-ordinated and positive manner.

Continued reference to the skills listed above (Fig. 1) will allow a child to be educated as a 'good mover' before and alongside the learning of specialised skills that may involve balls, bats, rackets and sticks. It will ensure that co-ordination, rhythm, balance and timing, factors common to all specialised movements, are constantly revisited as foundations and all children can be challenged but achieve success.

Developing fit and eager movers will go a long way to reversing some of the worrying 'trends' mentioned earlier!

## SAQ Junior Continuum

The SAQ Junior Continuum is the sequence and progression of components that make up the SAQ Junior Programme. The elements are:

1. Dynamic Flex™ Warm-Up – warming up on the move.

2. Mechanics – improving the quality of movement by learning 'how' to move.

3. Innervation – increasing the quickness and speed of movement.

4. Accumulation of potential – combining the quality and quickness of movements.

5. Explosion – improving the quickness and control of response.

6. Expression of potential – practical application of all movement skills.

7. Warm-down – returning the body back to normal and preparing for the next bout of physical activity.

The Continuum is flexible and allows each element to be used in isolation, for example in the early stages or when working with an individual or it can be used in its entirety when planning a lesson (see chapter 10). However the order indicated above does allow for a logical and effective development of fundamental movement.

## SAQ Equipment

SAQ Equipment adds variety and stimulus to your training session. Drill variations are unlimited and once mastered, the results achieved can be quite astonishing. Children of all ages and abilities enjoy the challenges presented to them when training with SAQ Equipment, particularly when introduced into PE lessons and sports training sessions.

When using SAQ Equipment, coaches, trainers and children must be aware of the safety issues involved and of the reduced effectiveness and potentially dangerous consequence of using inappropriate or inferior equipment.

The following pages introduce a variety of SAQ Equipment recommended for use in many of the drills detailed in this book and in other SAQ books.

## FAST FOOT LADDERS

are made of webbing with round, hard plastic rungs spaced approx. 18 inches apart; they come in sets of two pieces each measuring 15 feet. The pieces can be joined together or used as two separate ladders; they can also be folded over to create different angles for children to perform drills on. Fast Foot Ladders are excellent for improving agility and for the development of explosive fast feet.

## JUNIOR, MICRO AND MACRO V HURDLES

come in three sizes; Junior Hurdles measuring 4 inches, Micro V Hurdles measuring 7 inches, and Macro V Hurdles measuring 12 inches in height. They are constructed of a hard plastic and have been specifically designed as a safe freestanding piece of equipment. It is recommended that the hurdles be used in sets of 3–8 to perform the mechanics drills detailed later. They are ideal for practising running mechanics and low-impact plyometrics. They are particularly effective when used to develop lateral movement.

## SONIC CHUTES

are made from webbing (the belt), nylon cord and a lightweight cloth 'chute', the size of which may vary from 5 to 6 feet. The belt has a release mechanism that, when pulled, drops the chute so that the player can explode forwards. Sonic chutes are excellent for developing sprint endurance and have proved very popular with children.

## VIPER BELT

is a resistance belt specially made for high-intensity training. It has three stainless steel anchor points where a flexi-cord can be attached. The flexi-cord is made from surgical tubing with a specific elongation. The Viper Belt has a safety belt and safety fasteners; it is double-stitched and provides a good level of resistance. This piece of equipment is useful for developing explosive speed in all directions.

## SIDE-STEPPERS

are padded ankle straps that are connected together by an adjustable flexi-cord. They are especially useful for the development of lateral movements.

## REACTOR

is a rubber ball specifically shaped so that it bounces in unpredictable directions.

## OVERSPEED TOW ROPE

is made up of two belts and a 50 metre nylon cord pulley system. It can be used to provide resistance and is specifically designed for the development of express overspeed and swerve running.

## BREAK-AWAY BELT

is a webbing belt that is connected by Velcro-covered connecting strips. It is good for mirror drills and position-specific marking drills, breaking apart when one player gets away from the other. It is also very popular when used in fun games.

## STRIDE FREQUENCY CANES

are plastic, 4-foot canes of different colours that are used to mark out stride patterns.

## SPRINT SLED

is a metal sled with a centre area to accommodate different weights and a running harness that is attached by webbing straps of 8–20 metres in length.

## JELLY BALLS

are round, soft rubber balls filled with a water-based jelly-like substance. They come in different weights from 4 to 18lb. They differ from the old-fashioned medicine balls because they can be bounced with great force on to hard surfaces.

## HAND WEIGHTS

are foam-covered weights of 1.5–2.5lb. They are safe and easy to use both indoors and out.

## VISUAL ACUITY RING

is a hard plastic ring of approx 30 inches in diameter with 3 or 4 different coloured balls attached to it, all equally distributed around the ring. The ring helps to develop visual acuity and tracking skills when thrown and caught between the children.

## PERIPHERAL VISION STICK

is simple but very effective for the training of peripheral vision. It is about 4 feet long with a brightly coloured ball at one end. Once again this is effective for all children.

## BUNT BAT

a 4-foot stick with three coloured balls – one at each end and one in the middle. Working in pairs, player 1 holds the bat with two hands while player 2 throws a small ball or bean bag for player 1 to 'bunt' or fend off. This is effective for all children but particularly so for their hand–eye co-ordination.

## AGILITY DISC

an inflatable rubber disc 18 inches across. The discs are multipurpose but particularly good for proprioceptive and core development work (to strengthen the deep muscles of the trunk). They can be stood on, knelt on, sat on and lain on for the performance of all types of drills.

## SIDESTRIKE

a heavy duty platform with raised angled ends for foot placement. The ends are adjustable to accommodate different size athletes, the surface is padded to provide protection. It is a very effective piece of equipment for explosive footwork development, ideal for young goalkeepers, cricketers, and tennis players.

# How to use this book

This book is intended to assist parents who would like to help their child improve basic movements; teachers wishing to improve the whole range of fundamental movement patterns necessary to access the National PE Curriculum and sports teachers or coaches who are engaged in the development of specialised skills.

Once familiarity with the SAQ Continuum has been achieved it will be possible to dip into the various sections and plan lessons or sessions depending on the age, ability and aspirations of the children involved. Tremendous flexibility exists to match time available to performance requirements and in whether or not equipment is needed.

Where reference is made to Key Stage 1 (KS1) and Key Stage 2 (KS2) in schools, this refers to the age divisions, i.e. KS1 applying to children aged 5–7 and KS2 to ages 8–11.

Bearing in mind the research findings of Portwood (2003) for those working with early-years children (3+) many of the basic foundation movements mentioned will be very relevant to this population group (see example session, Appendix: Teaching and learning approaches).

Teachers working with classes of children on a regular basis will be able to use their in-depth knowledge of their performances to create differentiated practices and lesson plans (see example Chapter 10, Introductory lessons).

For teachers and coaches working with children in sport the programme is ideal for Long-Term Athletic Development (Bali) and provides crucial foundation work for multiskill training and development (see chapter10, Introductory lessons).

## Practices explained

Each practice is provided with an explanation of its aim, performance area used and equipment required and a description of how the children need to perform. There is a 'key teaching point' section which has been designed to help the reader learn the correct movements.

What you expect to see and what you actually get when a child performs can often be miles apart, so sections on 'what you might see' and 'solutions' have been provided to enable the observer to check and improve the performance. 'Sets and reps' (how many times) are indicated but these are just suggestions. When planning activity levels it is quality not quantity that is used as the guideline to judge the success of performance.

At the end of each page there is a section that provides variations and progressions that help stimulate the reader to provide new and interesting versions and ensure appropriate practice is given to meet the needs of each child (differentiation). Photographs and graphics are provided to help understanding and ensure that the practical application of the practices produces activity that is achievable, simple to organise and exhilarating to experience. Readers should feel free to use their imagination so that the activities meet the needs of the children and the facility and area being used.

How to apply the drills and practices to activity-specific situations is provided by way of example lesson sections and sample lesson plans and schemes of work.

Finally HEALTH AND SAFETY issues and recommendations are clearly indicated at the introduction of each part of the Continuum.

## Key

**The following symbols will be used in the drills throughout the book**

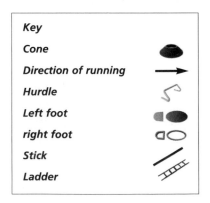

| Key | |
|-----|---|
| Cone | |
| Direction of running | |
| Hurdle | |
| Left foot | |
| right foot | |
| Stick | |
| Ladder | |

## *WARM-UP ON THE MOVE*

It is widely accepted that before engaging in intense or strenuous exercise the body should be prepared. The warm-up should achieve a change in a number of physiological responses in order that the body can work safely and effectively:

■ Increased body temperature, specifically core (deep) muscle temperature

■ Increased heart rate and blood flow

■ Increased breathing rate

■ Increased elasticity of muscular tissues

■ An activated neuro-muscular system (the message system that links the brain to the body)

■ Increased mental alertness

The warm-up should take a child from a rested state to the physiological state required for participation in the lesson/session that is to follow. The warm-up should gradually increase in intensity as the session goes on. It should also be functional in nature so as to prepare the body for the types of movements to be experienced. Additionally it should be fun and stimulating for the children so as to switch them on mentally.

## What is Dynamic Flex™?

Although not a standard definition, the following clearly explains what is involved in this method of warming up. A Dynamic Flex™ warm-up is a logical system of progressive and functional exercises that gradually warm and stretch muscle groups in preparation for physical activity. Dynamic Flex™ combines co-ordinated, rhythmic and graceful motions throughout a range of movement (ROM) specific to the activity (Finney 2004 SAQ® International).

Joints are mobilised and muscles synchronised through a natural mixture of contraction and relaxation which also helps stabilise the joints. Muscles work within their range of movement and in a multidimensional way similar to what might be experienced in the lesson to follow, i.e. matching preparation and performance. Because of the progressive and controlled nature of the movement performance, from small movements to larger and with controlled speed throughout, the stretch reflex mechanism of muscle contraction is not set off, thus avoiding concerns over muscle damage and soreness.

Interestingly, adult sportspeople, professional and amateur, and junior performers are now reporting, in increasing numbers, a reduction in soft tissue injury and muscle soreness since changing to a Dynamic Flex™ warm-up.

This method of warming up is a move away from the traditional method of beginning a PE lesson or sports training session, which has involved raising the pulse rate of children by jogging or running activities possibly involving grids and equipment, followed by a series of stretches that focus on the main muscle groups in the body. However, 'static' stretches like these are not the most appropriate when considering games or athletic movements. While static movements are common in gymnastics and dance and as such justify their inclusion as preparation for these specific activities, the vast majority of movements experienced by children are dynamic in nature thus leading to the conclusion that any preparatory activity should be functional and allow for the repeated contraction and stretching of muscle.

The Dynamic Flex™ warm-up focus should not detract from the need to develop flexibility as a vital component of health, fitness and sports performance. Research has made it clear that static stretching performs an essential role in improving flexibility. The question is where is it most appropriately experienced by children in the course of their lessons or training sessions?

In a school situation where time is at a premium, some stretching to recover in a cool-down and stretching as a focus during dance, gymnastics and health-related fitness units of work will enable children to learn this important feature of maintaining a fit and healthy body. (A unit of work is a number of lessons – typically six to eight – that covers a specific topic.)

As children are naturally flexible, when they enter a PE lesson or a training session they are already expecting to move. It seems logical therefore to take advantage of this natural exuberance, and to use the warm-up time not only to prepare them appropriately, but also to address immediately the issues mentioned previously about the lack of co-ordination, balance, rhythm and timing observed in children by many teachers and coaches.

With the movements listed below practised first from a stationary position, techniques developed carefully and practising the simple movements before the complex, much needed repetition of all these necessary foundations is achieved.

A Dynamic Flex™ warm-up is athletic and stretches muscles in motion. The focus is on motion, not on isolated muscles, and as such is of enormous benefit to children as they prepare for what should be an exhilarating experience.

A Dynamic Flex™ warm-up should not be seen to be 'ballistic' in nature.

Ballistic stretching can be defined as 'Bouncing and jerky movements in which one body segment is put in movement by active contraction of a muscle group and the momentum is then arrested by the antagonists (opposing muscle group) at the end of the range of motion' (De Vries 1986). Thus the antagonists are stretched by the ballistic movements of the agonists (prime moving muscles). The difference between a ballistic and a static stretch can be illustrated using the following: a typical example of a static stretch is an attempt to increase the hip flexion-knee extension range of motion by bending the knee forwards from an upright erect posture, keeping the knees extended and attempting to touch the toes with the fingers. The individual is instructed to keep the leg muscles passive and to maintain the stretch position for 15 to 30 seconds. The individual will feel that the range of motion is restricted by the tension that develops in the hamstring muscles. 'One variation of this exercise is to bounce up and down while attempting to touch the toes rather than sustaining one continuous stretch; the bouncing version is called ballistic stretching' (Enoka 1994).

For those wishing to read further into this subject specific research references are listed in the Bibliography and References.

## Health and Safety

■ Allow good spacing

■ Encourage controlled movements in every practice

■ Move through the activities in the recommended sequence

■ Emphasise care and correct technique when moving backwards

■ Discourage children from racing

## The Warm-up

Using the standard 10 m x 10 m grid marked out by marker dots placed at 1 m intervals for the channels and 2 m intervals for the length, follow the exercises as described in this chapter (see figure 1.1). Once foundation exercises are mastered, include variations and also vary the grid. This will help motivate and challenge the children.

## Dynamic Flex™ warm-up routines

A typical warm-up will last between 5 and 10 minutes depending on the age of the children and the length of the lesson/session.

All warm-ups progress from small to larger and from slow to faster movements with the emphasis throughout being the quality and control of each movement. Once basic mechanics are understood they should be constantly reinforced during the warm-up, e.g. good functional arm action and moving on the balls of the feet.

### Foundation Stage (4–5 years olds)

Organisation     On the spot Dynamic Flex™
Time             5 minutes

■ Jogging Forwards and Backwards

■ Walking on the Balls of the Feet (although not accurate the teaching point on the tiptoes may have to be used initially)

■ Lateral Walking on the Balls of the Feet

■ Lateral Running

■ Arm Roll and Jog

■ Static Lunges

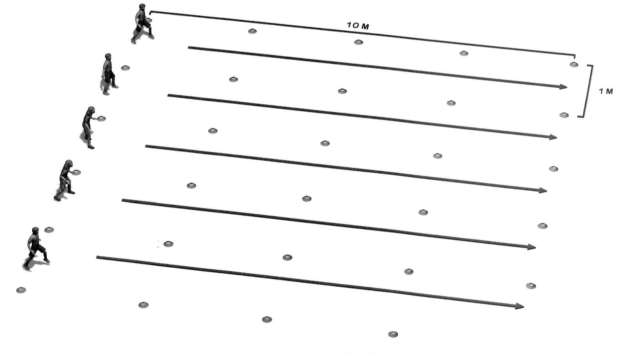

Figure 1.1 Standard grid

- Russian Walk

- 3 Steps Jog and 2 Small Jumps

## Key Stage 1 (5–7-year-olds)

Organisation     Standard Small Space Grid
Time             5 minutes

- Jogging Forwards and Backwards

- Walking on the Balls of the Feet

- Lateral Walking on the Balls of the Feet

- Lateral Running

- Ankle Flicks

- Lateral Ankle Flicks

- Small Skips

- Single-Knee Dead-Leg Lift

- Russian Walk

- Walking Lunge

- Walking Hamstring

- Lateral Jockeying

## Key Stage 2 (7–11 year olds)

Organisation     Standard Small Space Grid (first half)
Time             10 minutes

- Jogging Forwards and Backwards

- Jog and Hug

- Small Skip

- Wide Skip

- Single-Knee Dead-Leg Lift

- Knee-Aross Skip

- Lateral Knee-Across Skip

- Lateral Running

- Pre-Turn

- Carioca

- Hurdle Walk

- Russian Walk

- Walking Lunges

- Repeat again using Dynamic Flex™ out and Zigzag back organisation (see page 56).

# DRILL   *JOGGING FORWARDS AND BACKWARDS*

### Aim
To improve and teach forward and backward movements and the transfer from moving forwards to backwards; body and space awareness.

### Area/equipment
Use indoor or outdoor grid 10 metres in length.

### Description
Child moves forwards jogging and backwards with small steps in a slow controlled manner.

### Key teaching points
- Arms bent at 90-degree angle
- Work on the balls of the feet
- Before moving backwards widen base
- Push hips back slightly, chest leaning forwards
- Move back glancing to the sides
- Do not turn head behind

### What you might see
- Head turned behind with a backward lean from waist
- Falling back onto the heels

### Solutions
- Push hips back slightly, leaning slightly forwards
- Upright posture
- Practise peripheral vision using peripheral vision stick
- Keep on balls of the feet and keep chest forwards

### Sets and reps
2 x 10 metres forwards and backwards.
4 reps if moving from a spot.

### Variations/progressions
- Rotate core from side to side
- Jockey backwards alternating shoulder turn side to side

## DRILL | *WALKING –* *BEANBAGS/RUBBER RINGS ON HEAD*

### Aim
To improve posture and balance whilst walking.

### Area/equipment
Use indoor or outdoor area. Use marker spots, beanbag or rubber ring.

### Description
Child to move around the space in a slow rhythmical walk changing directions when arriving at another child and/or marker spot.

### Key teaching points
- Keep head up
- Achieve natural swing of arms
- Maintain upright posture
- Do not sink into the hips
- Maintain rhythmic walk

### What you might see
- Head down

- Shoulders slumped

- Unco-ordinated arms

### Solutions
- Get child to focus on an object on the horizon
- Head up, strong core, get child to breathe in, breathe out, hold the contraction, so they can breathe normally
- Arms to be held at 90 degrees, practise alternately driving them backwards

### Sets and reps
3 x 20 seconds walking.

### Variations/progressions
- Change direction more often
- Walk faster
- Play walking tag
- Step, squat down and up still maintaining posture and keeping beanbag/ring on head
- Lay out marker spots at different angles, child to move from spot to spot

# DRILL ARM ROLL AND JOG

### Aim
To improve shoulder mobility, balance and co-ordination, to increase body temperature and to develop positive foot-to-ground contact.

### Area/equipment
Use indoor or outdoor grid 10 metres in length. The width of the grid is variable depending on the size of the group.

### Description
Child covers length of grid by jogging forwards and backwards rolling the arms so that they go from below the waist to above the head in a rolling motion. Arms rolling forwards while jogging forwards and arms rolling backwards while jogging backwards.

### Key teaching points
- Keep arms slightly bent
- Keep off the heels
- Maintain upright posture
- Ensure adequate spacing between children
- Jog slowly backwards and be aware of others

### What you might see
- Arms rotated horizontally

- Sinking into the hips

### Solutions
- Child to brush arms past ears in a more vertical rotational movement
- Breathe in, breathe out lightly hold contraction so that normal breathing can occur

### Sets and reps
2 x 10 metres forwards and backwards.

### Variation/progression
Alternate arm rotation with one arm rolling forwards while the other rolls backwards.

# DRILL   ARM ROLL AND LATERAL JOG

### Aim
To improve shoulder mobility, balance and co-ordination; to increase body temperature and to develop positive lateral foot-to-ground contact.

### Area/equipment
Use indoor or outdoor grid 10 metres in length. The width of the grid is variable depending on the size of the group.

### Description
Child covers length of grid by jogging laterally, rolling the arms forwards so that they go from below the waist to above the head in a rolling motion.

### Key teaching points
- Keep arms slightly bent
- Keep off the heels
- Maintain upright posture
- Feet to be shoulder-width apart
- Ensure adequate spacing between children
- Jog slowly backwards and be aware of others

| What you might see | Solutions |
|---|---|
| Arms rotated horizontally | Child to brush arms past ears in a more vertical rotational movement |
| Sinking into the hips | Breathe in, breathe out lightly hold contraction so that normal breathing can occur |
| Crossing of feet | Keep hips square, ensure feet shoulder-width apart and use only short steps |
| Loss of balance | Drop heels to just above surface, perform drill more slowly |
| Stride too long | Work with feet shoulder-width apart, use marker dots to indicate recommended distance |
| Turning of hips | Look ahead, keep hips square |

### Sets and reps
2 x 10 metres forwards and backwards.

### Variation/progression
Alternate arm rotation with one arm rolling forwards while the other rolls backwards.

# DRILL   *SPOTTY DOGS*

### Aim
To improve shoulder and arm mobility, activate core muscles, improve balance and co-ordination and increase body temperature.

### Area/equipment
Use indoor or outdoor grid 10 metres in length. The width of the grid is variable depending on the size of the group.

### Description
Child covers length of grid by simultaneously chopping the legs and arms, left leg to left arm, right leg to right arm. Range of movement for the arm is from the side of the body up to the side of the face.

### Key teaching points
- Keep off the heels
- Arm action is a chop not a punch
- Land and take off on the balls of the feet
- Maintain upright posture
- Keep the head up

### What you might see
- Child landing flat-footed

- Jerky, unbalanced movements, poor co-ordination

- Child landing with 'stiff' straight legs

### Solutions
- Encourage the child to work on the balls of the feet by getting him/her to lean slightly forwards

- Develop a rhythm by getting the child to call out 'out, in, out, in' while they perform the drill, the calls coinciding with movement of the legs and arms

- Encourage bending at the knees

### Sets and reps
2 x 10 metres forwards

### Variation/progression
Child can perform the drill using opposite arms and legs.

# DRILL  JOG AND HUG

### Aim
To improve shoulder and chest mobility, balance and co-ordination, and to increase body temperature.

### Area/equipment
Use indoor or outdoor grid 10 metres in length. The width of the grid is variable depending on the size of the group.

### Description
Child covers length of grid by slowly jogging, bringing arms around the front of the body so that fingers can grip behind the opposite shoulder, alternating the arms over and under.

### Key teaching points
- Encourage squeeze
- Ensure adequate spacing between children
- Jog on the balls of the feet
- Maintain upright posture

### What you might see
- Trunk held too upright

- Running on the heels

### Solutions
- Child to tilt trunk slightly forwards and drop chin down closer to chest
- Child to lean body forwards, in order to push weight onto the balls of the feet

### Sets and reps
2 x 10 metres forwards.

### Variation/progression
Squeeze and then rotate the core turning from left to right, right to left.

# DRILL   *STAR JUMPS*

### Aim
To improve shoulder mobility, balance and co-ordination, and to develop positive foot-to-ground contact.

### Area/equipment
Use indoor or outdoor grid 10 metres in length. The width of the grid is variable depending on the size of the group.

### Description
Child works on the spot, simultaneously bringing arms out and above the head so that the insides of the arms are nearly touching the ears and hands come together above the head. Legs are split out in a jumping movement then brought together at the same time as the arms are brought back to the sides.

### Key teaching points
- Develop a rhythm
- Do not sink into the hips
- Stay tall
- Land and take off on the balls of the feet and not on the heels
- Ensure adequate spacing between children

### What you might see
- Sinking into the hips on landing


- Deep bending of the knees on landing

### Solutions
- Child to breathe in, out, breathe in again and hold the contraction so that they can breathe comfortably while performing the drill
- Child to land on the balls of the feet with firm knees and only a slight give

### Sets and Reps
10 star jumps.

### Variations/progressions
- Alternate bringing the arms out above the front of the head and then above the side of the head
- Perform star jumps moving forwards

## DRILL WALKING ON THE BALLS OF THE FEET

### Aim
To stretch shins and improve ankle mobility. To improve balance and co-ordination and to increase body temperature.

### Area/equipment
Use indoor or outdoor grid 10 metres in length. The width of the grid is variable depending on the size of the group.

### Description
Child covers length of grid by walking on the balls of the feet and returns to the start by repeating the drill backwards.

### Key teaching points
- Do not walk on the toes
- Keep off the heels
- Maintain correct arm mechanics
- Maintain an upright posture
- Squeeze buttocks together

### What you might see
- Child walking on toes



- Legs too wide apart

### Solutions
- Child to focus on walking on the balls of the feet, keeping head horizontal with the body leaning slightly forwards
- Feet to be shoulder-width apart, use marker dots for spacing if necessary

### Sets and reps
2 x 10 metres, 1 forwards and 1 backwards.

### Variation/progression
Child to perform drill with arms stretched out above head, which will challenge balance and core control.

# DRILL

## *LATERAL WALKING*
## *ON THE BALLS OF THE FEET*

### Aim
To stretch shins and improve ankle mobility, lateral balance and co-ordination. To increase body temperature.

### Area/equipment
Use indoor or outdoor grid 10 metres in length. The width of the grid is variable depending on the size of the group.

### Description
Child covers length of the grid by walking on the balls of the feet sideways and returns to the start by repeating the drill moving back in the opposite sideways direction.

### Key teaching points
- Do not bring feet completely together
- Do not cross feet
- Do not walk on the toes
- Keep off the heels
- Maintain correct arm mechanics
- Maintain an upright posture
- Keep hips square
- Feet to be shoulder-width apart
- Keep head up

### What you might see
- Crossing of feet
- Loss of balance
- Strides too long

- Bringing the feet together

### Solutions
- Keep hips square
- Keep hips square
- Work with feet shoulder-width apart

- Work with feet shoulder-width apart

### Sets and reps
2 x 10 metres, 1 with left shoulder and 1 with right shoulder leading.

### Variation/progression
Hold arms above the head.

# DRILL ANKLE FLICKS

## Aim

To stretch calves and improve ankle mobility. To improve balance, co-ordination and rhythm of movement. To prepare for good foot-to-floor contact. To increase body temperature.

## Area/equipment

Use indoor or outdoor grid 10 metres in length. The width of the grid is variable depending on the size of the group.

## Description

Child covers length of grid in a skipping motion where the balls of the feet plant then flick up towards the shin. Child should be seen to move in a rhythmic, bouncing manner. Return to the start by repeating the drill backwards.

## Key teaching points

- Work off the balls of the feet, not the toes
- Practise the first few steps on the spot before moving off
- Maintain correct arm mechanics
- Maintain an upright posture

## What you might see

- Poor plantar/dorsiflex range of movement (raising and lowering of the toes)
- Jerky, unrhythmic movement

## Solutions

- Child to pull toes towards shin on the upward flick
- Use calls 'up, down' or 'one, two' to help with rhythm

## Sets and reps

2 x 10 metres, 1 forwards and 1 backwards.

## Variation/progression

Perform the drill with stop–start variations.

## DRILL    *LATERAL ANKLE FLICKS*

### Aim
To stretch calves and improve lateral ankle mobility. To improve balance, co-ordination and rhythm of movement while moving sideways. To prepare for good foot-to-floor contact. To increase body temperature.

### Area/equipment
Use indoor or outdoor grid 10 metres in length. The width of the grid is variable depending on the size of the group.

### Description
Child covers length of the grid in a skipping motion where the balls of the feet plant then flick up towards the shin while moving laterally. Child should be seen to move in a rhythmic, bouncing manner. Return to the start by repeating the drill in the opposite lateral direction.

### Key teaching points
- Work off the balls of the feet, not the toes
- Practise the first few steps on the spot before moving off
- Maintain correct arm mechanics
- Maintain an upright posture
- Feet to be shoulder-width apart

### What you might see / Solutions

| What you might see | Solutions |
|---|---|
| Feet coming too close together | Work with feet shoulder-width apart |
| Poor plantar/dorsiflex range of movement (raising and lowering of the toes) | Child to pull toes towards shin on the upward flick |
| Jerky, unrhythmic movement | Use calls 'up, down' or 'one, two' to help with rhythm |

### Sets and reps
2 x 10 metres, 1 forwards and 1 backwards.

### Variation/progression
Perform the drill with stop–start variations.

# DRILL  *SMALL SKIPS*

### Aim
To improve lower leg flexibility and ankle mobility. To improve balance, co-ordination and rhythm and to develop positive foot-to-ground contact. To increase body temperature.

### Area/equipment
Use indoor or outdoor grid 10 metres in length. The width of the grid is variable depending on the size of the group.

### Description
Child covers length of the grid in a low, skipping motion and returns to the start by repeating the drill backwards.

### Key teaching points
- Raise knee to an angle of about 45–55 degrees
- Work off the balls of the feet
- Maintain correct arm mechanics
- Maintain an upright posture
- Maintain a good rhythm

| What you might see | Solutions |
|---|---|
| ■ Knees lifted too high | ■ Child to focus on the knee not coming any higher than the waistband |
| ■ Poor rhythm | ■ Same as above |

### Sets and reps
2 x 10 metres, 1 forwards and 1 backwards.

### Variation/progression
Perform the drill in a long figure-of-eight.

# DRILL   *LATERAL SMALL SKIPS*

### Aim
To improve lower leg flexibility and lateral ankle mobility. To improve balance, co-ordination and rhythm and to develop positive lateral foot-to-ground contact. To increase body temperature.

### Area/equipment
Use indoor or outdoor grid 10 metres in length. The width of the grid is variable depending on the size of the group.

### Description
Child covers length of grid in a low, lateral, skipping motion and returns to the start by repeating the drill in the opposite lateral direction.

### Key teaching points
- Raise knee to an angle of about 45–55 degrees
- Feet to be shoulder-width apart
- Push off the trailing foot
- Work off the balls of the feet
- Maintain correct arm mechanics
- Maintain an upright posture
- Maintain a good rhythm

### What you might see
- Lead foot over-reached



- Knees lifted too high


- Poor rhythm

### Solutions
- Encourage pushing off from trailing foot not pulling from lead foot; remind child that if a car breaks down you push it not pull it
- Child to focus on the knee not coming any higher than the waistband
- Same as above

### Sets and reps
2 x 10 metres, 1 forwards and 1 backwards.

### Variation/progression
Perform the drill with occasional turns from left to right shoulder while moving down the grid.

# DRILL WIDE SKIP

### Aim

To improve hip and ankle mobility. To improve balance, co-ordination and rhythm. To increase body temperature.

### Area/equipment

Use indoor or outdoor grid 10 metres in length. The width of the grid is variable depending on the size of the group.

### Description

Child covers length of grid by skipping. The feet should remain wider than shoulder-width apart and the knees face outwards at all times. Return to the start by repeating the drill backwards.

### Key teaching points

- Keep off the heels
- Maintain correct arm mechanics
- Maintain an upright posture
- Do not take the thigh above a 90-degree angle

### What you might see

- Landing on flat feet

- Arms and elbows held in too tight to the body

### Solutions

- Child to lean slightly forwards, and is shown how to focus with the eyes on an object on the floor 15–20 metres ahead
- Encourage arm drive. Inside of the wrist should brush pockets, thumb should come up to side of face

### Sets and reps

2 x 10 metres, 1 forwards and 1 backwards.

### Variation/progression

Move from forwards to backwards every 3/4 skips moving in the same direction.

# DRILL  LATERAL WIDE SKIP

### Aim
To improve hip and lateral ankle mobility. To improve balance, co-ordination and rhythm while moving sideways. To increase body temperature.

### Area/equipment
Use indoor or outdoor grid 10 metres in length. The width of the grid is variable depending on the size of the group.

### Description
Child covers length of the grid by laterally skipping. The feet should remain wider than shoulder-width apart and the knees face outwards at all times. Return to the start by repeating the drill in the opposite lateral direction.

### Key teaching points
- Keep off the heels
- Feet should be wider than shoulder-width apart
- Maintain correct arm mechanics
- Maintain an upright posture
- Do not take the thigh above a 90-degree angle

### What you might see
- Landing on flat feet



- Arms and elbows held in too tight to the body



- Head held too far back

### Solutions
- Child to lean slightly forwards, and is shown how to focus the eyes on an object on the floor 15–20 metres ahead
- Encourage arm drive. Inside of wrist should brush pockets, thumb should come up to side of face
- Focus on a horizontal point that keeps the head level

### Sets and reps
2 x 10 metres, 1 forwards and 1 backwards.

### Variation/progression
Perform the drill with occasional turns from left to right shoulder while moving down the grid.

# DRILL  KNEE OUT SKIP

## Aim
To stretch the inner thigh and improve hip mobility. To develop an angled knee drive, balance, co-ordination and rhythm. To increase body temperature.

## Area/equipment
Use indoor or outdoor grid 10 metres in length. The width of the grid is variable depending on the size of the group.

## Description
Child covers length of grid in a skipping motion. The knee moves from the centre of the body to a position outside the body before returning to the central position. Return to the start by repeating the drill backwards.

## Key teaching points
- Feet start in a linear position and move outwards as the knee is raised
- Work off the balls of the feet
- The knee is to be pushed, not rolled, out and back
- Maintain correct arm mechanics
- The movement should be smooth, not jerky

## What you might see
- Landing on the heel

- Leaning back too far

## Solutions
- Focus on landing on the balls of the feet, trunk leaning forwards
- Keep head slightly dipped towards chest

## Sets and reps
2 x 10 metres, 1 forwards and 1 backwards.

## Variation/progression
Perform the drill slowly while rotating 360 degrees, knee out every 90 degrees.

## DRILL  *LATERAL KNEE OUT SKIP*

### Aim
To stretch the inner thigh and improve lateral hip mobility. To develop an angled knee drive, balance, co-ordination and rhythm while moving sideways. To increase body temperature.

### Area/equipment
Use indoor or outdoor grid 10 metres in length. The width of the grid is variable depending on the size of the group.

### Description
Child covers length of the grid in a lateral skipping motion. The knee moves from the centre of the body to a position outside the body before returning to the central position while moving sideways. Return to the start by repeating the drill in the opposite lateral direction.

### Key teaching points
- Feet start in a lateral position and move outwards as the knee is raised
- Push from the trailing foot
- Work off the balls of the feet
- The knee is to be pushed, not rolled, out and back
- Maintain correct arm mechanics
- The movement should be smooth, not jerky

### What you might see
- Landing on the heel

- Leaning back too far

- Head held too far back

### Solutions
- Focus on landing on the balls of the feet, trunk leaning forwards
- Keep head slightly dipped towards chest
- Focus on an object just below child's horizon

### Sets and reps
2 x 10 metres, 1 forwards and 1 backwards.

### Variation/progression
3 skips out, 1 back.

## DRILL  SINGLE-KNEE DEAD-LEG LIFT

### Aim
To improve buttock flexibility and hip mobility. To isolate the correct 'running cycle' motion for each leg.

### Area/equipment
Use indoor or outdoor grid 10 metres in length. The width of the grid is variable depending on the size of the group.

### Description
Child covers length of grid by bringing the knee of one leg quickly up to a 90° position. The other leg should remain as straight as possible with a very short lift away from the ground throughout the movement. The ratio should be 1:4, i.e. 1 lift to every 4 steps. Work one leg on the way down the grid and the other on the return.

### Key teaching points
- Do not raise knees above 90 degrees
- Strike the floor with the ball of the foot
- Keep the foot in a linear position
- Maintain correct running mechanics

### What you might see
- Both knees being lifted



- Jerky form and rhythm



- Knee lift angled either out or across the body

### Solutions
- Child to focus on one side only and perform the drill at a walking pace, i.e. walk, lift, walk, lift
- Use marker dots to help rhythm, work on this drill in the mechanics phase
- Perform drill with the arm on the knee-lift side held out in a linear position with the palm of the open hand facing downwards, bring knee up to touch the palm of the hand and return to the ground

### Sets and reps
2 x 10 metres, 1 forwards and 1 backwards.

### Variation/progression
Vary the lift ratio, e.g. 1:2.

## DRILL   *HIGH KNEE-LIFT SKIP*

### Aim
To improve buttock flexibility and hip mobility. To increase the range of motion (ROM) over a period of time. To develop rhythm. To increase body temperature.

### Area/equipment
Use indoor or outdoor grid 10 metres in length. The width of the grid is variable depending on the size of the group.

### Description
Child covers length of grid in a high skipping motion and returns to the start by repeating the drill backwards.

### Key teaching points
- Thigh to be taken past 90 degrees
- Work off the balls of the feet
- Maintain a strong core
- Maintain an upright posture
- Control the head by looking forwards at all times
- Maintain correct arm mechanics

### What you might see
- Child landing on the heels

- Inconsistency of knee-lift (different heights)

### Solutions
- Child to lean forwards and focus on the balls of the feet
- Knee to be raised just above waistband, and drill performed at walking pace so that the range of movement can be practised

### Sets and reps
2 x 10 metres, 1 forwards and 1 backwards.

### Variation/progression
Perform the drill laterally.

# DRILL  LATERAL HIGH KNEE-LIFT SKIP

### Aim
To improve buttock flexibility and lateral hip mobility. To increase the range of motion (ROM) over a period of time. To develop rhythm whilst moving sideways. To increase body temperature.

### Area/equipment
Use indoor and outdoor grid 10 metres in length. The width of the grid is variable depending on the size of the group.

### Description
Child covers length of grid in a high, lateral skipping motion. returns to the start and repeats the drill in the opposite lateral direction.

### Key teaching points
- Thigh to be taken past 90 degrees
- Feet starting-point to be shoulder-width apart
- Work off the balls of the feet
- Maintain a strong core
- Maintain an upright posture
- Control the head by looking forwards at all times
- Maintain correct arm mechanics

### What you might see
- Child landing on the heels

- Inconsistency of knee-lift (different heights)

- Turned hips

### Solutions
- Lean forwards and focus on the balls of the feet
- Knee to be raised just above waistband, and drill performed on the spot or at walking pace so that the range of movement can be practised
- Hips to be kept square at all times. Drill can be performed with child's hands on hips holding them square

### Sets and reps
2 x 10 metres, 1 forwards and 1 backwards.

### Variations/progressions
- 2 out, 1 back
- Alternate shoulders, left to right every few steps

# DRILL KNEE-ACROSS SKIP

### Aim
To improve outer hip flexibility and hip mobility over a period of time. To develop balance and co-ordination. To increase body temperature.

### Area/equipment
Use indoor or outdoor grid 10 metres in length. The width of the grid is variable depending on the size of the group.

### Description
Child covers length of the grid in a skipping motion where the knee comes across the body, and returns to the start by repeating the drill backwards.

### Key teaching points
- Do not force an increased ROM
- Work off the balls of the feet
- Maintain a strong core
- Maintain an upright posture
- Control the head by looking forwards at all times
- Use the arms primarily for balance

### What you might see
- Too high-a-knee lift

- Skipping on heels

### Solutions
- Knee should not go above waistband
- Child to lean forwards slightly, weight to be transferred onto the balls of the feet

### Sets and reps
2 x 10 metres, 1 forwards and backwards.

### Variation/progression
3 forwards, 2 backwards.

# DRILL    LATERAL KNEE-ACROSS SKIP

### Aim
To improve outer hip flexibility and lateral hip mobility over a period of time. To develop balance and co-ordination while moving sideways. To increase body temperature.

### Area/equipment
Use indoor or outdoor grid 10 metres in length. The width of the grid is variable depending on the size of the group.

### Description
Child covers length of grid in a lateral skipping motion where the knee comes across the body, and returns to the start by repeating the drill in the opposite lateral direction.

### Key teaching points
■ Do not force an increased ROM
■ Arms can be pushed across body
■ Work off the balls of the feet
■ Maintain a strong core
■ Maintain an upright posture
■ Control the head by looking forwards at all times
■ Use the arms primarily for balance

### What you might see
■ Too high a knee-lift

■ Skipping on heels

### Solutions
■ Knee should not go above waistband
■ Child to lean forwards slightly, weight to be transferred onto the balls of the feet

### Sets and reps
2 x 10 metres, 1 forwards and backwards.

### Variation/progression
After every 3 sideways skips turn and lead with other shoulder.

# DRILL   *LATERAL RUNNING*

### Aim

To develop economic knee drive, stretch the side of the quadriceps and prepare for an efficient lateral running technique. To increase body temperature.

### Area/equipment

Use indoor or outdoor grid 10 metres in length. The width of the grid is variable depending on the size of the group.

### Description

Child covers length of grid with the left or right shoulder leading, taking short, lateral steps, and returns with the opposite shoulder leading.

### Key teaching points

■ Keep the hips square
■ Work off the balls of the feet
■ Do not skip
■ Do not let the feet cross over
■ Maintain an upright posture
■ Do not sink into the hips or fold at the waist
■ Do not overstride – use short, sharp steps
■ Maintain correct arm mechanics

| What you might see | Solutions |
| --- | --- |
| ■ Feet crossing or being brought together | ■ Encourage child to focus on working with feet shoulder-width apart |
| ■ Skipping sideways | ■ Child to focus on stepping not skipping motion |
| ■ No arm movement or arms by the side | ■ Child to hold a foam ball in each hand and practise correct arm drive techniques by brushing the side of the body with the ball and bringing the ball up to the side of the face |

### Sets and reps

2 x 10 metres, 1 leading with the left shoulder and 1 with the right.

### Variation/progression

Practise lateral-angle zigzag runs.

# DRILL    PRE-TURN

## Aim

To prepare the hips for a turning action without committing the whole body. To increase body temperature and improve body control.

## Area/equipment

Use indoor or outdoor grid 10 metres in length. The width of the grid is variable depending on the size of the group.

## Description

Child covers length of grid by performing a lateral movement. The heel of the trailing foot is moved to a position almost alongside the lead foot. Just before the feet come together, the lead foot is moved away laterally. Return to the start by repeating the drill but leading with the opposite shoulder.

## Key teaching points

- The trailing foot must not cross the lead foot
- Work off the balls of the feet
- Maintain correct arm mechanics
- Maintain an upright posture
- Do not sink into the hips or fold at the waist
- Do not use a high knee-lift, the angle should be no more than 45 degrees

## What you might see

- Crossing of feet

- Leading leg raised and stepping forwards instead of trailing leg

- Hips turned

## Solutions

- Child to focus on stepping not skipping motion, use marker dots to indicate where feet should be placed in pre-turn stepping
- Child to use the arm of the leading side to press down on the thigh as a reminder that this leg remains straighter
- Child encouraged to stand tall with head up and breathe in and out, then hold contraction

## Sets and reps

2 x 10 metres, 1 leading with the left shoulder and 1 with the right.

# DRILL **CARIOCA**

## Aim
To improve hip mobility and speed, which will increase the firing of nerve impulses over a period of time. To develop balance and co-ordination while moving and twisting. To increase body temperature.

## Area/equipment
Use indoor or outdoor grid 10 metres in length. The width of the grid is variable depending on the size of the group.

## Description
Child covers length of grid by moving laterally. The trailing foot crosses in front of the body and then moves around to the back. Simultaneously, the lead foot does the opposite. The arms also move across the front and back of the body.

## Key teaching points
- Start slowly and build up the tempo
- Work off the balls of the feet
- Keep the shoulders square
- Do not force the ROM
- Use the arms primarily for balance

## What you might see
- Sinking into the hips

- Co-ordination problem i.e. unable to put leg trailing the front leg
- Arms swung too fast or not at all

## Solutions
- Child to stand tall, with head up, breathe in and out then hold contraction
- Practise slowly, go through the drill at walking pace

- Allow the arms to do what comes naturally

## Sets and reps
2 x 10 metres, 1 leading with the left leg and 1 with the right.

## Variation/progression
Perform the drill laterally with a partner (mirror drills) i.e. one initiates or leads the movement while the other attempts to follow.

# DRILL  STATIC LUNGES

### Aim
To stretch the inner thighs and gluteals (buttocks). To develop balance and co-ordination, to perfect movement before introducing walking lunges. To increase body temperature.

### Area/equipment
Use indoor or outdoor grid or marker spots to stand on.

### Description
From a standing position the child performs a static lunge. The front leg should be bent with a 90-degree angle at the knee and the thigh in a horizontal position. The back leg should also be at a 90-degree angle but with the knee touching the ground and the thigh in a vertical position. The drill is alternated from one side to the other.

### Key teaching points
- Stable starting position, feet to be hip-width apart
- Maintain width of base when stepping forwards
- Keep trunk upright
- Do not push front knee forwards over foot, keep shinbone vertical
- Use opposite arm to leg

### What you might see
- Stepping and narrowing base
- Bending forwards at waist

- Uncontrolled arm movement

### Solutions
- Use a marker spot to step onto
- Keep head up and trunk upright
- Hold a ball in two hands

### Sets and reps
Alternate 2–4 times on each leg.

### Variations/progressions
- Step backwards
- Step to either side
- Step forwards at an angle

# DRILL SIDE LUNGE

### Aim
To stretch the inner thighs and gluteals (buttocks). To develop balance and co-ordination. To increase body temperature.

### Area/equipment
Use indoor or outdoor grid 10 metres in length. The width of the grid is variable depending on the size of the group.

### Description
Child covers length of grid by performing lateral lunges: taking a wide, lateral step and simultaneously lowering the gluteals towards the ground; returns to the start with the opposite shoulder leading.

### Key teaching points
- Do not bend at the waist or lean forwards
- Try to keep off the heels
- Maintain a strong core and keep upright
- Use the arms primarily for balance

### What you might see
- Child leaning forwards

### Solutions
- Keep spine in an upright aligned position by keeping head up and chin maintained on a horizontal plane

### Sets and reps
2 x 10 metres, 1 leading with the left shoulder and 1 with the right.

### Variation/progression
Rotate body after each lunge to face the opposite direction.

# DRILL   HAMSTRING BUTTOCK FLICKS

### Aim
To stretch the front and back of thighs and improve hip mobility. To increase body temperature.

### Area/equipment
Use indoor or outdoor grid 10 metres in length. The width of the grid is variable depending on the size of the group.

### Description
Child covers length of grid by moving forwards alternating leg flicks where the heel moves up towards the buttocks. On the returns to the start repeat the drill but work backwards.

### Key teaching points
- Start slowly and build up the tempo
- Work off the balls of the feet
- Maintain an upright posture
- Do not sink into the hips
- Try to develop a rhythm

### What you might see
- Knee raised up towards front of body

- Hands held at the back above the top of the thighs

### Solutions
- Thigh to remain vertical to the ground with movement starting from below the knee. Practise the leg flick while standing still, using a wall or a partner for stability; get child to look down and observe the movement required

- Explain to the child we move with hands in front not behind our backs

### Sets and reps
2 x 10 metres, 1 forwards and 1 backwards.

### Variation/progression
Perform the drill as above but flick the heel to the outside of the buttocks.

# DRILL  *LATERAL HAMSTRING BUTTOCK FLICKS*

### Aim
To stretch the front and back of thighs and improve lateral hip mobility. To increase body temperature.

### Area/equipment
Use indoor or outdoor grid 10 metres in length. The width of the grid is variable depending on the size of the group.

### Description
Child covers length of grid by moving laterally alternating leg flicks where the heel moves up towards the buttocks, and returns to the start repeating the drill in the opposite lateral direction.

### Key teaching points
- Start slowly and build up the tempo
- Feet to be shoulder-width apart
- Work off the balls of the feet
- Maintain an upright posture
- Do not sink into the hips
- Try to develop a rhythm

### What you might see
- Knee raised up towards front of body

- Hands held at the back above the top of the thighs

### Solutions
- Thigh to remain vertical to the ground with movement starting from below the knee; practise the leg flick while standing still, using a wall or a partner for stability; get child to look down and observe the movement required
- Explain to child that we move with hands in front not behind our backs

### Sets and reps
2 x 10 metres, 1 forwards and 1 backwards.

### Variation/progression
Incorporate different arm movement, i.e. pushing out or punching up while performing the drill.

# DRILL    *HEEL TO INSIDE OF THIGH SKIP*

### Aim
To stretch the hamstrings, groin and gluteals. To improve balance and co-ordination and to increase body temperature.

### Area/equipment
Use indoor or outdoor grid 10 metres in length. The width of the grid is variable depending on the size of the group.

### Description
Child covers length of grid in a skipping motion where the heel of one leg comes up almost to touch the inside thigh of the opposite leg. Imagine there is a football on a piece of string that is hanging centrally just below your waist and you are trying to kick it with alternate heels. Return backwards.

### Key teaching points
- Start slowly and build up the tempo
- Work off the balls of the feet
- Maintain an upright posture
- Maintain a strong core throughout
- Use arms for balance

### What you might see
- Confusion between high knee skip and heel to inside thigh skip

### Solutions
- Heel of lifted leg to be directed towards the inside of the groin. Heel can touch the inside of the thigh as a cue for correct range of movement.

### Sets and reps
2 x 10 metres, 1 forwards and 1 backwards.

### Variation/progression
Perform drill with hands on head, this is good for posture.

# DRILL   *HURDLE WALK*

### Aim
To stretch inner and outer thighs and to increase ROM. To develop balance and co-ordination and increase body temperature.

### Area/equipment
Use indoor or outdoor grid 10 metres in length. The width of the grid is variable depending on the size of the group.

### Description
Child covers length of the grid by walking in a straight line and lifting alternate legs as if going over high hurdles, and return to the start repeating the drill backwards.

### Key teaching points
- Try to keep the body square as the hips rotate
- Feet to be shoulder-width apart
- Work off the balls of the feet
- Maintain an upright posture
- Do not sink into the hips or bend over at the waist
- Imagine that you are actually stepping over a barrier

### What you might see
- The anchored foot is flat while the other leg is raised;. this will cause a poor range of movement

### Solutions
- Child to focus on working off the ball of the foot that is anchored; practise by getting the child to stand with feet shoulder-width apart and rise up off the heels onto the ball of the foot, hold for a second and then return to the starting positions; repeat for 20–30 times. This will provide kinaesthetic feedback to the child as to what it feels like to be on the balls of the feet

### Sets and reps
2 x 10 metres, 1 forwards and 1 backwards.

### Variation/progression
Can be performed on the spot.

# DRILL   RUSSIAN WALK

## Aim

To stretch the back of the thighs. To improve hip mobility and ankle stabilisation. To develop balance and co-ordination and increase body temperature.

## Area/equipment

Use indoor or outdoor grid 10 metres in length. The width of the grid is variable depending on the size of the group.

## Description

Child covers length of grid by performing a walking march with a high, extended step. Imagine that the aim is to scrape the sole of your shoe down the front of a door or fence. Return to the start by repeating the drill backwards.

## Key teaching points

- Lift the knee before extending the leg
- Work off the balls of the feet
- Try to keep off the heels, particularly on the back foot
- Keep the hips square
- Toes pulled towards shin so that they point vertically to the sky

## What you might see

- Toe pointing out horizontally not vertically

## Solutions

- Child to pull the toe towards the shin, and practise the Russian Walk on the spot before introducing forward walking

## Sets and reps

2 x 10 metres, both forwards.

## Variations/progressions

- Perform the drill backwards but do not reverse the leg motion
- Perform the drill laterally

| DRILL | *WALKING LUNGE* |
|---|---|

### Aim
To stretch the front of hips and thighs. To develop balance and co-ordination and increase body temperature.

### Area/equipment
Use indoor or outdoor grid 10 metres in length. The width of the grid is variable depending on the size of the group.

### Description
Child covers length of grid by performing a walking lunge. The front leg should be bent with a 90-degree angle at the knee and the thigh in a horizontal position. The back leg should also be at a 90-degree angle but with the knee touching the ground and the thigh in a vertical position. During the lunge the child will bring both arms above the head to activate core muscles. Return to the start by repeating the drill backwards.

### Key teaching points
- Try to keep the hips square
- Maintain a strong core and keep upright
- Maintain good control
- Persevere with backward lunges – these are difficult to master
- Trunk to be in an upright position

### What you might see
- Poor overall ability to perform the drill properly
- Poor balance and control

- Stride too short causing inability to lunge properly

### Solutions
- Practise drill slowly on the spot
- Overstriding can cause this. Ensure that child bends knee at 90 degrees and the thigh is in a horizontal position; use marker dots to indicate length of lunge
- Focus on knee bend of 90 degrees and the thigh is in a horizontal position; practise drill slowly on the spot if poor form continues

### Sets and reps
2 x 10 metres, 1 forwards and 1 backwards.

### Variations/progressions
- Perform the drill with handweights
- Perform the drill while catching and passing a ball in the down position
- Alternate arms above the head, one up and one down

# DRILL    *WALKING HAMSTRING*

### Aim
To stretch the backs of the thighs.

### Area/equipment
Use indoor or outdoor grid 10 metres in length. The width of the grid is variable depending on the size of the group.

### Description
Child covers length of the grid by extending the lead leg, heel first, on the ground and rolling onto the ball of the foot and sinking into the hips, while keeping the spine in a linear position. Walk forwards and repeat on the opposite leg; continue in this manner alternating the lead leg. For comfort cross arms.

### Key teaching points
- Keep the spine straight
- Do not bend over
- Control the head by looking forwards at all times
- Work at a steady pace, do not rush

| What you might see | Solutions |
|---|---|
| Head down, leaning forwards | Child to keep chin up and focus on something horizontally in line with the eyes |
| Bent at the waist | Hips to be kept square, trunk and spine to remain in an upright position |

### Sets and reps
2 x 10 metres, 1 forwards and 1 backwards.

### Variation/progression
Perform on the spot.

## DRILL  *LATERAL WALKING HAMSTRING*

### Aim
To stretch the backs of the thighs laterally.

### Area/equipment
Use indoor or outdoor grid 10 metres in length. The width of the grid is variable depending on the size of the group.

### Description
Child covers length of grid laterally by extending the lead leg, heel first, on the ground and rolling onto the ball of the foot and sinking into the hips, while keeping the spine in a linear position. Walk sideways and repeat on the opposite leg; continue in this manner alternating the lead leg. For comfort cross arms.

### Key teaching points
- Keep the spine straight
- Keep feet shoulder-width apart
- Do not bend over
- Control the head by looking forwards at all times
- Work at a steady pace, do not rush

### What you might see
- Head down, leaning forwards

- Bent at the waist

### Solutions
- Child to keep chin up and focus on something horizontally in line with the eyes
- Hips to be kept square, trunk and spine to remain in an upright position

### Sets and reps
2 x 10 metres, 1 forwards and 1 backwards.

### Variation/progression
Work laterally performing the drill on the same leg then change to the other leg on the way back.

## DRILL  ICE SKATING

### Aim
To improve hip and ankle mobility, lateral foot control, balance and - co-ordination.

### Area/equipment
Use indoor or outdoor grid 10 metres in length. The width of the grid is variable depending on the size of the group.

### Description
Child leans forwards slightly and swings the arms across the body while sidestepping from left to right foot like an ice skater. Ensure good spacing and start a group going all in the same direction.

### Key teaching points
- Keep head up
- Do not sink into hips or lean over
- Try to land on the balls of the feet

### What you might see
- Stepping too far or losing control
- Head down on landing

### Solutions
- Use a channel of marker spots to land on
- Focus eyes on a point in the distance

### Sets and reps
2 x 10 metres.

### Variations/progressions
- Alternate from short steps to long steps
- Repeat ice skating backwards

# *STANDARD SMALL SPACE GRID*

### Aim
To warm-up dynamically in a small area.

### Area/equipment
Indoor or outdoor restricted space and marker dots.

### Description
Standard 10 metres grid split up into 2 starting and finishing lines,
ideal for organizing small squads and groups of children.

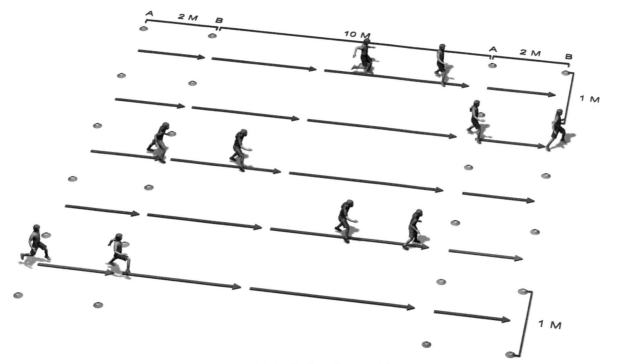

Figure 1.2 Standard small space grid

## DRILL ON THE SPOT DYNAMIC FLEX™

### Aim
To perform Dynamic Flex™ on the spot; ideal for restricted areas and space, including keep fit studios and small school halls.

### Area/equipment
Indoor or outdoor area, marker dots spaced with a 2-metre circumference.

### Description
Drills are performed on the spot within the space provided.

### Variation/progression
Additional movements can be introduced after each drill, getting children to move to a different spot.

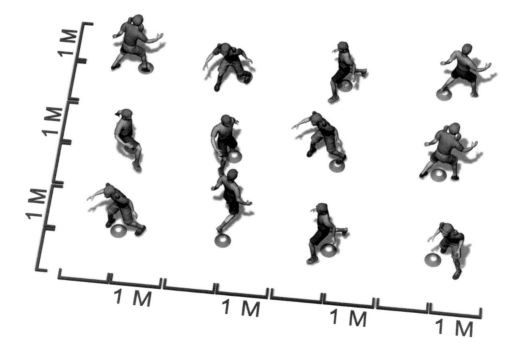

Figure 1.3 On the spot Dynamic Flex™

| DRILL | DYNAMIC FLEX™ OUT, ZIGZAG BACK |
| --- | --- |

### Aim
To stimulate and motivate child with a variety of movement patterns.

### Area/equipment
Mark out an indoor or outdoor grid 10 metres in length with markers placed at 2-metre intervals. The width of the grid is variable depending on the size of the group. Place a line of markers on each side of the grid about 2 metres away with 1 metre between each marker.

### Description
Perform Dynamic Flex™ down the grid with the group splitting around the end markers to return on the outside of the grid. On reaching the markers the child should zigzag back through them.

### Key teaching point
The timing is crucial: the child should be constantly on the move.

### Sets and reps
Children can perform the entire Dynamic Flex™ warm-up in this manner.

### Variation/progression
Replace the markers on the outside of the grid with Fast Foot Ladder or hurdles.

Figure 1.4  Out, Zigzag back

# DRILL    SPLIT GRID

### Aim
To improve ball control and passing skills.

### Area/equipment
Mark out an indoor or outdoor grid 10 metres in length with an additional 5 metres on the end (use different coloured markers). The width of the grid is variable depending on the size of the group. Place a ball for each child who will have just completed his/her Dynamic Flex™ drill.

### Description
Perform Dynamic Flex™ down the grid over the first 10 metres; on reaching the additional 5 metres area perform beanbag or ball skills up and back over it, i.e. catching and juggling (manipulation skills). On completing the skills, pass the beanbag or ball to the child coming on, who will have just completed his/her Dynamic Flex™ drill.

### Key teaching points
- The timing is crucial: the child should be constantly on the move
- Children should communicate with one another, e.g. when passing the ball

### Sets and reps
Children can perform the entire Dynamic Flex™ warm-up in this manner.

### Variation/progression
Vary the manipulation skills and the objects passed between the children.

Figure 1.5 Split grid

| **DRILL** | *CIRCLE GRID* |
|---|---|

### Aim
To stimulate and motivate the child by adding difficulty to the movements, creating further challenge.

### Area/equipment
Mark out an indoor or outdoor grid with a circle of markers 15 metres in diameter and a centre circle 5 metres in diameter. The diameter of the circle is variable depending on the size of the group you are working with.

### Description
Perform Dynamic Flex™ around the outside of the circle, changing directions forwards and backwards. Then the child can perform other drills, i.e. the walking hamstring, while moving from the outer to the centre circle.

### Key teaching point
Timing and change of direction are very important.

### Sets and reps
Children can perform the entire Dynamic Flex™ warm-up in this manner.

### Variation/progression
Introduce manipulation skills.

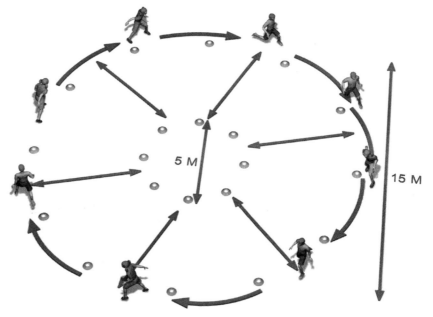

**Figure 1.6 Circle grid**

# DRILL | STAR GRID

### Aim
To stimulate and motivate the child by adding difficulty to the movements, creating further challenge.

### Area/equipment
Mark out an indoor or outdoor grid with markers, forming an 8-point star. The points will measure 5 metres to the centre circle. Markers will be placed for the inner as well as outer points of the star, which will provide 16 starter points. The points of the star can be increased depending on the size of the group.

### Description
Perform Dynamic Flex™ from the outside to the inside point of the star. Then work from the inside to the outside point of the star.

### Key teaching point
Timing and change of direction are very important at the point and end of the star

### Sets and reps
Children can perform the entire Dynamic Flex™ warm up in this manner.

### Variation/progression
Introduce manipulation skills.

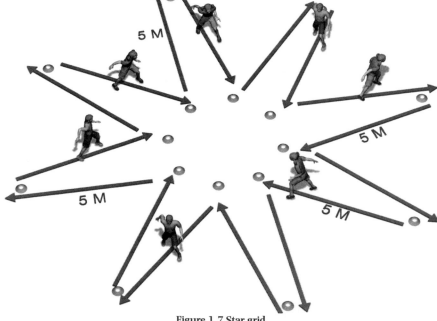

Figure 1.7 Star grid

## DRILL | *ZIGZAG GRID*

### Aim
To stimulate and motivate the child by adding difficulty to the movements, creating further challenge.

### Area/equipment
Use indoor or outdoor grid with markers 1 metre apart forming a 1-metre channel; every 2 metres along the grid the markers move sideways to create a zigzag (see diagram).

### Description
Perform Dynamic Flex™ down the channel following the zigzag pattern.

### Key teaching point
Timing and change of direction are very important.

### Sets and reps
Children can perform the entire Dynamic Flex™ warm up in this manner.

### Variation/progression
Introduce manipulation skills.

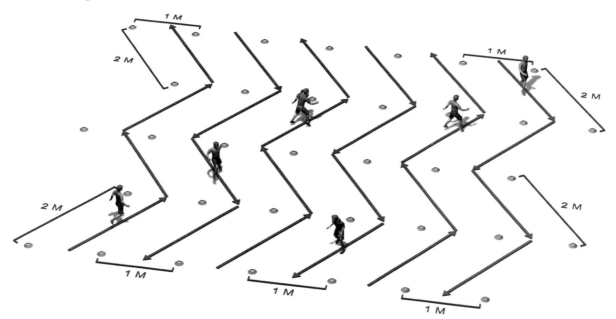

Figure 1.8 Zigzag grid

## *IMPROVING THE QUALITY OF MOVEMENT*

One of the most damaging assumptions made by those working with children is that running and moving correctly is something that occurs naturally through play. Talented children who make movement such as running and dodging look easy are apparent in every lesson and sporting club, but a real cause for concern is that increasingly teachers and coaches are reporting that these children are in the minority. To neglect the quality of even simple 'natural' movements in PE lessons and training sessions is to ignore the potential in all children.

How often are comments heard about children in regard to their inability to move, i.e. 'too slow', 'flat footed', 'runs on the heels', 'flaps the arms', 'poorly co-ordinated'? All children, whatever their age, can improve their ability to move, accelerate, dodge, twist and turn by practising and applying the correct movement mechanics.

In this section there will be a focus on arm mechanics, running form, acceleration and deceleration, lift mechanics, posture, lateral and backwards movement, jumping, and twisting and turning. Once again co-ordination, rhythm, balance and timing are factors that are constantly revisited and developed.

When these techniques have been learned they should be repeated and reinforced in every activity experienced, from the movements found in the Dynamic Flex™ warm-up, to all remaining activities and drills covered in the Continuum, and to all sports-specific skills that are subsequently taught. They will form solid foundations on which sports-specific movements, for example 'jockeying' in soccer, moving backwards in netball and moving sideways in tennis can be developed.

Once the drills are introduced in isolation it is important then to put them into the context of the relevant activity; for example, if linear running is the focus of the drill, once practised and improved it can be combined with catching and throwing a ball in order to develop 'passing and moving' in a game situation.

The movement checklist that follows sets out the key points that need to be taught when assisting children to begin to run, accelerate, maintain a fast stride pattern, decelerate, run sideways, turn and jump.

## Arm Mechanics

- Elbows should be held at 90 degrees

- Hands and shoulders should be relaxed

- The insides of the wrists should brush against the pockets

- The hands should move from the buttock cheeks to the chest or head

## Lift Mechanics

Coaching children to get their knees up high, particularly in the first few metres of the acceleration phase, only makes them slower. Using high knee-lift during the acceleration phase has the negative effect of minimizing force development; therefore not enough power is produced to propel the body forwards in an explosive action. During the first few metres of acceleration short, sharp steps are required. These steps generate a high degree of force which takes the body from a stationary position into the first controlled explosive steps.

The first phases of acceleration and reacceleration for all movement patterns are crucial. Look and listen for the following in a child's initial acceleration strides:

- 45-degree knee-lift

- Foot-to-floor contact with the ball of the foot

- Front of the foot stays in a linear position

- Knees coming up in a vertical line

- Foot-to-floor contact making a tapping noise, not a thud or slap

- The foot and knee should not splay in or out, or power will not be transferred correctly

- Keep off the heels

- On the lift, the foot will transfer from pointing slightly down to pointing slightly up

## Posture

Posture is a crucial part of all movements required for activity including sprinting, jumping and turning. The spine should be kept as straight as possible at all times. This means that a child who has jumped into the air and then has to run into a space, needs to transfer to the correct running form as quickly as possible. Running with a straight spine does not mean running bolt upright, you can keep your spine straight using a slight lean forwards. What is to be avoided is a child running while sinking into the hips, which looks like being folded up in the middle, or sinking too deep when landing after jumping, because this prevents instant effective transfer of power. Some children have a tendency to move too many parts of the body all at the same time when trying to run. This causes instability, inadequate use of energy and poor transfer of power, so that the ability to move efficiently is severely restricted. Core control will help stabilise the child's movement, and is therefore another important factor in developing and utilising a strong posture. Core development and maintenance for children is very important. A simple rule prior to and throughout the performing of all the drills in this book is: engage the core muscles by simply breathing in, breathing out and then breathing in again; try to maintain this feeling throughout the exercise – not forgetting to breathe normally! This will help prevent your pelvic wall from moving around, which causes a loss of power, and will also protect the lower back, hamstrings and girdle area from injury.

## Mechanics for Deceleration

The ability of a child to stop quickly, change direction and accelerate away when dodging and sidestepping while playing 'tag', for instance, can be practised: do not leave it to chance, include it in your sessions.

- Posture – lean back. This alters the angle of the spine and hips which controls foot placement, and causes foot contact with the ground to transfer to the heel, which acts like a brake.

- Fire the arms – by firing the arms quickly, the energy produced will increase the frequency of heel contact to the ground. Think of it like pressing harder on the brakes in a car.

The running techniques described in this chapter cover basic mechanics for children where running, jumping and turning are all important parts of the movement. They are developed through the use of hurdles, stride frequency canes and running technique drills.

## Mechanics for change of direction including lateral and turning movements

### LATERAL SIDESTEP

Do not use a wide stance as this will decrease the potential for power generation as you attempt to push off or away. Do not pull with the leading foot but rather push off the back foot. Imagine that your car has broken down and that you need to move it to a service station – would you pull it? No you would push it. Ensure that a strong arm drive is used at all times but particularly during the push-off phase.

### MAKING A 180–DEGREE TURN – THE DROP STEP

Most children use too many movements in making a 180-degree turn. Many jump up on the spot first then take 3 or 4 steps to make the turn, others will jump up and perform the turn in the air with a complete lack of control. When practised, the drop-step turn looks seamless and is far quicker.

For a right shoulder turn the child starts by opening up the right groin and simultaneously transferring the weight onto the left foot. The right foot is raised slightly off the ground and, using a swinging action, is moved around to the right to face the opposite direction. The right foot is planted and the child drives/pushes off the left foot, remembering to use a strong arm drive. He/she should not overstretch on the turn. Children may find it helpful initially to tell themselves to 'turn and go'. With practice children will develop an efficient and economic seamless turn.

### JUMPING

- Both elbows should be held at 90 degrees

- Hands should be moved from buttock cheeks to above the head both at the same time

- Jump from the balls of the feet

- Land on the balls of the feet

- Keep trunk tall and hips leaning forwards slightly

- On landing, do not sink into the hips, use slight knee bend

## Health and Safety

- Allow 'eyes down' runs until a basic level of proficiency is achieved, to avoid children tripping

- Allow one runner to clear at least 3 hurdles before the next runner goes

- Fallen hurdles should be repositioned immediately, facing the correct way

- Create clear working grids to avoid collisions

- Monitor quantities of effort to allow adequate recovery between repetitions

# Observing quality movement checklist for children

## RUNNING – STARTING POSITION

| Correct | Incorrect | Solution |
|---|---|---|
| **Feet**<br>■ Shoulder-width apart<br>■ Too close<br>■ On the ball<br>■ Straight - linear | ■ Too wide<br>■ On the toes<br>■ On the heels<br>■ Weight outside or inside<br>■ Pointing in<br>■ Splayed out | ■ Use chalk marks or marker spots on the surface to indicate best position<br>■ Slight lean forwards on the ball of the foot<br>■ Heels off the ground<br>■ Position feet in a straight – linear position<br>■ Use straight lines to position feet<br>■ Use chalk to mark around the foot on hard surfaces so the outline can be used to ensure correct positioning |
| **Arms**<br>■ Held ready 90 degrees at elbow<br>■ One forward, one back<br>■ Relaxed | ■ Arms by the side<br>■ Shoulders shrugged with arms too high<br>■ Tight and restricted | ■ Provide constant feedback on arm technique<br>■ Practise holding arms in correct position, then accelerate arms as if starting to run; perform Partner arm drive drills (see p. 61)<br>■ Loop string/elastic band around index finger and thumb and point of elbow to hold correct position of 90 degrees |
| **Hips**<br>■ Need to be high – tall – slightly forwards | ■ Sunk<br>■ Twisted | ■ Hold head tall and upright<br>■ Hold stomach in, focus on keeping the hips high and lean forwards slightly in the running direction<br>■ Keep chin off chest<br>■ Focus on good linear body position |
| **Head**<br>■ Held high<br>■ Eyes forwards | ■ Held down, turned<br>■ Looking up | ■ Imagine you are looking over a fence that comes up to your nose<br>■ Pick an object in the distance and focus on it |

## RUNNING – ACCELERATION PHASE

| Correct | Incorrect | Solution |
|---|---|---|
| **Hand**<br>■ Fingertips gently touching | ■ Soft (most common)<br>■ Droopy<br>■ Tightly closed | ■ Hold post-it note or something similar between index finger and thumb |
| **Arm action**<br>■ Fast<br>■ 90 degree angle at elbow<br>■ Hand above shoulder<br>■ One forward, one back behind hips | ■ Slow to medium | ■ Perform Partner arm drive drills (see p. 61)<br>■ Use short, sharp sets of on-the-spot, fast arm bursts<br>■ Use light handweights for 8–9 seconds then perform contrast arm drives as quickly as possible afterwards |
| **Arm drive**<br>■ Chin to waist<br>■ Wrist or hand firm | ■ Arms across body<br>■ Forearm chop<br>■ At the side<br>■ Held in stiff, angled position | ■ Perform Partner arm drive drills (see p. 61)<br>■ Brush the inside of the wrist against waistband, then touch thumb to chin<br>■ Loop string/elastic band, around index finger and thumb and point of elbow, then perform arm drives<br>■ Perform arm drive drill in front of mirror for feedback<br>■ Perform Buttock bounces (see p. 63)) |
| **Head**<br>■ Held high<br>■ Keep up<br>■ Eyes forwards | ■ Held down<br>■ Turned<br>■ Looking up<br>■ Looking from side to side | ■ Imagine you are looking over a fence that comes up to your nose<br>■ Pick an object in the distance and focus on it |
| **Body position – Trunk**<br>■ Tall<br>■ Strong | ■ Sunk<br>■ Soft<br>■ Bent | ■ Head up; hold stomach in, hips high, slightly forwards and square |
| **Foot action**<br>■ Active – plantar flex (toe down)<br>■ dorsiflex (toe up) | ■ Flat<br>■ Heel first to touch ground<br>■ Inactive plantar (toe down)/ dorsiflex (toe up) | ■ Focus on balls of feet<br>■ Remove built up heeled shoes<br>■ Practise plantar/dorsiflex skip<br>■ Ensure there is a slight forward body lean<br>■ Keep head up; do not sink into the hips |

Running – ACCELERATION PHASE (continued)

| Correct | Incorrect | Solution |
|---|---|---|
| **Heel**<br>■ Raised | ■ Down, contacting ground first | ■ Focus on balls of feet<br>■ Remove built-up heeled shoes<br>■ Take rolled-up cloth or paper into a small ball, slightly larger than a marble; place in shoe under heels |
| **Hips**<br>■ Tall<br>■ Square<br>■ Up/forwards<br>■ Firm<br>■ Still | ■ Bent<br>■ Sunk<br>■ Turned | ■ Hold stomach in, focus on keeping the hips square to the running direction<br>■ Practise buttock bounces (see p. 63) |
| **Knees**<br>■ Linear<br>■ Below waist<br>■ Foot just off ground<br>■ Drive forwards | ■ Across body<br>■ Splayed<br>■ Too high with foot too high off ground | ■ Practise Dead-leg run (see p. 65).<br>■ Teacher/coach to place hands above where knees should go, practise bringing the knees up to the hand by running on the spot<br>■ Use coloured tape, stick from above the knee in a straight line to below knee, either on skin or clothing. The tape should now go across the centre of the knee cap. Now perform on-the-spot running drills in front of the mirror, focus on keeping the coloured tape in a straight line |
| **Relaxation**<br>■ Relaxed<br>■ Calm<br>■ Comfortable | ■ Tense<br>■ Too loose<br>■ Distracted | ■ Imagine accelerating quickly with power and grace, but feeling calm and relaxed<br>■ Control breathing |

## RUNNING – AFTER ACCELERATION (PLANING–OUT–PHASE)

| Correct | Incorrect | Solution |
|---|---|---|
| **Stride length**<br>■ Medium for individual | ■ Too long<br>■ Too short | ■ Use marker spots or stride frequency canes to mark out correct distances of stride length |
| **Stride frequency**<br>■ Balanced for individual | ■ Too quick<br>■ Too slow | ■ Perform Partner arm drive drills (see p. 61)<br>■ Use marker spots or stride frequency canes to mark out correct distances of stride length |
| **Arm action**<br>■ Fast<br>■ 90-degree angle at elbow<br>■ Hand above shoulder, behind hips | ■ Slow to medium | ■ Perform Partner arm drive drills (see p. 61)<br>■ Use short, sharp sets of on-the-spot fast arm bursts<br>■ Use light handweights for 8–9 seconds then perform contrast arm drives as quickly as possible afterwards |
| **Arm drive**<br>■ Chin to waist<br>■ Hand or wrist firm<br>■ Eyes forwards | ■ Arms across body<br>■ Forearm chop<br>■ At the side<br>■ Held in stiff, angled position | ■ Perform Partner arm drive drills (see p. 61)<br>■ Brush the inside of the wrist against waist band, then touch thumb to chin<br>■ Loop string/elastic bands, around index finger and thumb and point of elbow, then perform arm drives<br>■ Perform Buttock bounces (see p. 63) |
| **Body position – trunk**<br>■ Tall<br>■ Strong | ■ Sunk<br>■ Bent | ■ Hold head up and stomach in; hips high, slightly forwards and square |
| **Foot action**<br>■ Active – plantar flex (toe down)<br>■ Dorsiflex (toe up) | ■ Flat<br>■ Heel first to touch ground<br>■ Inactive plantar (toe down)/ dorsiflex (toe up) | ■ Focus on balls of feet<br>■ Practise plantar/dorsiflex skip<br>■ Ensure there is a slight forward body lean<br>■ Keep head up; do not sink into the hips |
| **Relaxation**<br>■ Relaxed<br>■ Calm | ■ Tense<br>■ Too loose | ■ Imagine accelerating quickly with power and grace, but feeling calm and relaxed |

## LATERAL STEPPING AND RUNNING

| Correct | Incorrect | Solution |
| --- | --- | --- |
| **Foot action** | | |
| ■ Work off balls of feet | ■ On the heels<br>■ Flat-footed | ■ Lean forwards slightly even when stepping sideways<br>■ Provide constant feedback to keep off heels<br>■ Keep hips tall and strong; this helps control power and prevent flat-footed weight transfer |
| ■ Feet shoulder-width apart | ■ Too wide<br>■ Too close<br>■ Crossed<br>■ Pointing in<br>■ Splayed out | ■ Use marker spots to indicate best foot position for lateral stepping<br>■ Practise stepping slowly at first, build up speed gradually |
| ■ Drive off trailing foot | ■ Reach with leading foot<br>■ Flat-footed<br>■ On heels<br>■ Feet pointing in or splayed | ■ Use marker spots to indicate best foot positions<br>■ Use coloured tape, stick on shoes from tongue to toe in straight line; working in front of mirror, focus on keeping the lines on the foot straight<br>■ Place taped ball of paper under heel of each foot<br>■ Use angled boards to step off |
| **Hips** | | |
| ■ Firm<br>■ Controlled<br>■ Square<br>■ High | ■ Soft<br>■ Twisted<br>■ Angled<br>■ Leaning too far forwards<br>■ Bent at the waist<br>■ Sunk | ■ Hold head tall<br>■ Hold stomach in<br>■ Focus on keeping hips square |
| **Arm action** | | |
| ■ Elbows at 90-degree angle<br>■ Fast and strong drive | ■ Arm across the body<br>■ No arm drive at all<br>■ Arms too tight and restricted<br>■ Arms moving forwards but not driving backwards behind the hips | ■ Perform Partner arm drive drills (see p. 61), practise moving sideways<br>■ Provide constant positive feedback |
| **Trunk** | | |
| ■ Strong and firm<br>■ Lean slightly forwards | ■ Too upright<br>■ Leaning too far forwards<br>■ Bent at the waist<br>■ Leaning back | ■ Head facing forwards and stills, touch thumb to chin<br>■ Hold stomach in<br>■ Slight knee bend only |

## LATERAL TURNING – 90–DEGREE (PRE–TURN)

| Correct | Incorrect | Solution |
|---|---|---|
| **Feet**<br>■ Shoulder-width apart | ■ Together<br>■ Too wide<br>■ Crossed | ■ Use chalk marks or marker spots to indicate best starting and finishing position |
| **On the turn**<br>■ Keep feet shoulder-width apart<br>■ Work on balls of feet<br>■ High | ■ Together<br>■ Crossed<br>■ Too wide apart<br>■ Onto the heels<br>■ Onto the toes | ■ Hold head tall<br>■ Hold stomach in<br>■ Focus on keeping hips square<br>■ Use chalk marks or marker spots to indicate best starting and finishing position<br>■ Practise single turn in front of mirror |
| **Foot drive**<br>■ Drive off trailing foot<br>■ Fast and strong drive | ■ Reach forwards<br>■ Jump on the spot<br>■ Rock back on heels | ■ Keep trunk firm<br>■ Get children to say the word, 'push' on the drive 'off' on the turn, either in their heads or out loud<br>■ Practise lateral sidesteps slowly then build up speed<br>■ Maintain good arm drive |
| **Hips**<br>■ High, slightly forwards and square<br>■ Hip before knee | ■ Low and sunk<br>■ Angled not square<br>■ Trunk leaning too far forwards or too upright | ■ Keep hips firm, tall and leaning forwards<br>■ Use arm drive with hips to assist turn<br>■ Keep hips square when turning<br>■ Practise turns slowly at first |
| **Head**<br>■ Keep up<br>■ Off the chest<br>■ Eyes forwards<br>■ Head and hip work simultaneously during turn | ■ Floppy<br>■ Down<br>■ Angled<br>■ Back | ■ Pick two distant objects, one in front of you, the other in the direction you are turning to. Initially focus on the object in front, on the turn refocus on the second object |

## 180-DEGREE TURN

| Correct | Incorrect | Solution |
|---|---|---|
| **Initial movement**<br>■ Seamless<br>■ Movement smooth, no punctuations<br>■ Sequence is drop, step and go $(1-2-3)$ | ■ Jump up<br>■ Step back<br>■ Twist | ■ Practise drop step, the opening of the leg to point in the direction of the turn; the trailing foot then pushes off<br>■ Practise saying out loud 'drop, step and go'<br>■ Practise slowly at first, gradually developing speed<br>■ Practise facing a wall, so when you turn the back step is prevented<br>■ Practise turn in front of mirror<br>■ Use video of turn |
| **Feet**<br>■ Shoulder-width apart | ■ Together<br>■ Too wide<br>■ Crossed | ■ Use chalk marks or marker spots to indicate best starting and finishing position |
| **Arm drive**<br>■ Elbows at 90-degree angle<br>■ Fast and strong drive<br>■ Hand above shoulder, behind hips | ■ Arm across the body<br>■ No arm drive at all<br>■ Arms too tight and restricted<br>■ Arms moving forwards but not driving backwards behind the hips | ■ Perform Partner arm drive drills (see p. 61); practise moving sideway<br>■ Provide constant positive feedback |
| **Head**<br>■ Up<br>■ Eyes forwards | ■ Down<br>■ Angled<br>■ Turned | ■ Pick two distant objects, one in front of you, the other behind; initially focus on the object in front, on the turn refocus on the second object |
| **Hips**<br>■ High, slightly forwards and square<br>■ Hip before knee | ■ Low and sunk<br>■ Angled not square<br>■ Trunk leaning too far forwards or too upright | ■ Keep hips firm, tall and leaning forwards<br>■ Use arm drive with hips to assist turn<br>■ Keep hips square when turning<br>■ Practise turns slowly at first |

## JUMPING

| Correct | Incorrect | Solution |
|---|---|---|
| **Arm drive**<br>■ Arms 90 degrees working together from behind the hips to above the head<br>■ Sequence is drop, step and go (1 – 2 – 3) | ■ No arm movement<br>■ Arms not working together<br>■ One arm used | ■ Practise with a balloon: hold the balloon in front, below the chest, with both hands, and then throw the balloon over the back of the head<br>■ Once balloon drill is perfected introduce the throwing of the balloon with a jump |
| ***Pre-jump hips***<br>■ Tall, slightly forwards | ■ Bent<br>■ Sunk (most common)<br>■ Crossed | ■ Keep hips firm, tall and leaning forwards<br>■ Keep hips square when jumping<br>■ Hold head up and stomach in |
| **Feet at take off**<br>■ On balls of the feet | ■ Flat-footed<br>■ On the heels<br>■ On the toes | ■ Provide constant feedback to keep off heels<br>■ Keep hips tall and strong<br>■ Use a small round stick or old book half an inch in thickness; place under both heels so that weight is forced onto the ball of the foot, and practise jumping in this position |
| **Feet when landing**<br>■ On balls of the feet<br>■ Weight equally balanced on both feet when possible | ■ On the toes<br>■ Heels<br>■ Unbalanced | ■ Practise multiple bunny hops landing on the balls of the feet, so that correct foot-to-ground contact is practised<br>■ Place taped ball of paper under heel of each foot |
| **Trunk**<br>■ Tall, hips leaning forwards slightly<br>■ Firm and relaxed | ■ Sunk<br>■ Bent at the waist<br>■ Twisted | ■ Breathe in and hold stomach firm; keep head high |
| **Hips**<br>■ Firm<br>■ Tall<br>■ Slightly leaning forwards | ■ Hip low and sunk<br>■ Angled not square<br>■ Trunk leaning too far forwards or too upright | ■ Keep hips firm, tall and leaning forwards.<br>■ Use arm drive with hips to assist control<br>■ Keep hips square when landing<br>■ Practise landing by simply jumping off a step or small box |

## DECELERATION

| Correct | Incorrect | Solution |
|---|---|---|
| **Arms**<br>■ Keep at 90 degrees<br>■ Increase speed of drive on deceleration | ■ Slow arm drive<br>■ No arm drive<br>■ Arms dropped by the sides | ■ Provide feedback as soon as deceleration commences of 'drive arms'<br>■ Loop string/elastic band around index finger and thumb and point of elbow to hold correct position of 90 degrees<br>■ Use light handweights that are released at the deceleration phase |
| **Feet**<br>■ Shorten stride to smaller steps | ■ Maintain long strides<br>■ Too wide<br>■ Crossed | ■ Use coloured canes or marker dots or a short piece of outdoor Fast Foot Ladder at the deceleration phase |
| **Head**<br>■ Slightly raised above horizontal plane<br>■ Eyes up | ■ Chin down on chest<br>■ Head turned to one side | ■ Prior to deceleration phase focus on an object in the distance that is slightly higher than the horizon, requiring the head to be brought up<br>■ Teacher/coach to call 'head up' as deceleration phase begins |
| **Hips**<br>■ Lean back | ■ Remain forwards<br>■ Lopsided<br>■ Sunk | ■ Focus on bringing the head up; this will change the angle of the hips |
| **Trunk**<br>■ Brought upright | ■ Remained tilted forwards<br>■ Bent | ■ Get children to focus on:<br>1. Head up<br>2. Trunk up<br>3. Hips back<br>Work on this combination during deceleration |
| **Heel**<br>■ Transfer weight to heel<br>■ Heel first | ■ On the toes<br>■ Too much weight forwards on the balls of the feet | ■ Get children to focus on:<br>1. Head up<br>2. Trunk up<br>3. Hips back<br>Work on this combination during deceleration; this will impact on the spine, causing the heel to come down on the ground first for deceleration |

# DRILL

## RUNNING FORM EXERCISE –
## ARM MECHANICS – ARM DRIVE

### Aim
To perfect and practise correct arm technique for running.

### Area/equipment
Indoor or outdoor area. Individual space to perform exercise.

### Description
Children stand with space around them so that they can perform the drill safely. Elbows are held at 90 degrees, hands are relaxed, slowly the child brushes the inside of the wrist on the side of the body so that the elbow is driven back, the hand is then moved to the side of the face and then returned back to drive the elbow back again. Hips are kept square and head held up. Start very slowly and gradually build up speed of the arm drive.

### Key teaching points
- Arms should not move across the body
- Forearms should not be chopped up and down as if hitting a drum
- Hands and shoulders should be relaxed
- Hips should be kept firm not turned or twisted
- Head should be kept up on a horizontal plane
- Maintain a slight lean forwards onto the balls of the feet
- Core should be firm, not sinking into the hips

### Sets and reps
3 sets of 10 reps on each arm, 30 seconds recovery between each set.

### Variation/progression
Child to hold foam balls in each hand, balls to be brushed against the side of the body (pocket area) and to the side of the cheek.

| **DRILL** | *RUNNING FORM –*<br>*ARM MECHANICS – PARTNER DRILLS* |

## Aim
To perfect the correct arm technique for running in sport.

## Area/equipment
Child to work with a partner.

## Description
Child stands with partner behind him/her. Partner should hold the palms of his/her hands in line with the child's elbows, fingers pointing upwards. Child fires the arms as if sprinting so that the elbows smack into partner's palms.

## Key teaching points
- Arms should not move across the body
- Elbows should be at 90 degrees
- Hand and shoulders should be relaxed
- The insides of the wrists should brush against the pockets
- ROM – the hands should move from buttock cheeks to chest or head
- Encourage speed of movement to hear the smack

## Sets and reps
3 sets of 10 reps, with 30 seconds recovery between each set.

## Variation/progression
Use beanbags or foam ball in each hand.

### ARM MECHANICS –
# DRILL    ARM DRIVE FOR JUMPING

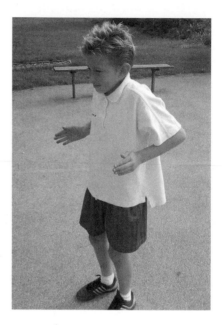

### Aim
To perfect correct arm technique for jumping.

### Area/equipment
Indoor or outdoor area. Individual space to perform exercise.

### Description
Child stands in space large enough to perform the drill safely. Elbows are held at 90 degrees and hands are relaxed. Simultaneously both arms are slowly driven back so that they brush the sides of the body with the sides of the wrists. Then at the same time they are brought forwards to touch the side of the cheeks and then driven back slowly to the original position. Gradually increase the speed of the movement.

### Key teaching points
■ Arms should not move across the body
■ Arms move together through an arch from hips to ears
■ Hands should be relaxed
■ Head held up
■ Use only a slight bend of the knees

### Sets and reps
3 sets of 10 reps, with 30 seconds recovery between each set.

### Variation/progression
Use a beanbag or foam ball in each hand.

# *ARM MECHANICS – BUTTOCK BOUNCE*

### Aim
To develop explosive arm drive.

### Area/equipment
Suitable ground surface.

### Description
Child sits on the floor with his/her legs straight out in front, and fires the arms rapidly in short bursts. The power generated should be great enough to raise the buttocks off the floor in a bouncing manner.

### Key teaching points
- Arms should not move across the body
- Elbows should be at 90 degrees
- Hands and shoulders should be relaxed
- The insides of the wrists should brush against the pockets
- ROM – the hands should move from buttock cheeks to chest or head
- Encourage speed of movement to hear the smack

### Sets and reps
2 sets of 4 reps; each rep is 6–8 explosive arm drives with 1 minute recovery between each set.

### Variation/progression
Use a beanbag or foam ball in each hand.

# DRILL

## LEG MECHANICS –
## KNEE-LIFT DEVELOPMENT

### Aim
To develop and practise correct knee-lift technique for running.

### Area/equipment
Indoor or outdoor area. Fence, wall or partner to lean against.

### Description
Child leans against wall with one arm, the other arm is angled down so that the palm (facing down) is just below the waist out in front of the body. Bring knee up to the palm of hand and then down, ensuring that the ball of the foot and not the heel hits the ground. This is repeated on both sides of the body.

### Key teaching points
- Start slowly gradually increase speed
- Knee to be brought up in a straight line
- Ball of the foot, not any other part, to hit the ground
- Child should look ahead
- Maintain a slight body lean
- No sinking or twisting of the hips

### Sets and reps
2 sets of 10 reps on each leg, 30 seconds recovery between each set.

### Variations/progressions
- Hold arm out above the waist: this will vary the height of the knee-lift
- Use mats, carpet, foam so that the foot strikes the material, providing a different feedback to the child

# DRILL  *RUNNING FORM – DEAD-LEG RUN*

### Aim
To develop a quick knee-lift and the positive foot placement required for effective sprinting.

### Area/equipment
Indoor or outdoor area. Using hurdles, marker dots or sticks, place approximately 8 obstacles in a straight line at 2-foot intervals. Place a marker dot 1 metre from each end of the line to mark a start and finish.

### Description
Child must keep the outside leg straight in a locked position. The inside leg moves over the obstacles in a cycling motion while the outside leg swings along just above the ground.

### Key teaching points
- Bring the knee of the inside leg up to just below 90 degrees
- Point the toe upwards
- Bring the inside leg back down quickly between the hurdles
- Increase the speed when the technique has been mastered
- Maintain correct arm mechanics
- Maintain an upright posture and a strong core
- Keep the hips square and stand tall

### Sets and reps
1 set of 6 reps, 3 leading with the left leg and 3 with the right.

### Variation/progression
Place several different-coloured markers 2 metres from the last hurdle at different angles. As the child leaves the last hurdle the teacher/coach nominates a marker for the child to accelerate to.

Figure 2.1 Dead-leg run

| DRILL | RUNNING FORM – PRE-TURN |
|---|---|

### Aim
To educate and prepare the hips, legs and feet for effective and quick turning without fully committing the whole body.

### Area/equipment
Indoor or outdoor area. Using hurdles, marker dots or sticks, place about 8 obstacles in a straight line at 2-foot intervals. Place a marker dot 1 metre from each end of the line to mark a start and finish.

### Description
Child moves sideways along the line of obstacles, just in front of them, i.e. not travelling over them. The back leg (following leg) is brought over the hurdle to a position slightly in front of the body so that the heel is in line with the toe of the leading foot. As the back foot is planted, the leading foot moves away. Repeat the drill leading with the opposite leg.

### Key teaching points
- Stand tall and do not sink into the hips
- Do not allow the feet to cross over
- Keep the feet shoulder-width apart as much as possible
- The knee-lift should be no greater than 45 degrees
- Maintain correct arm mechanics
- Maintain an upright posture
- Keep the hips and shoulders square
- Work both the left and right sides

### Sets and reps
1 set of 6 reps, 3 leading with the left shoulder and 3 with the right.

### Variations/progressions
- Place several different-coloured markers 2 metres from the last hurdle at different angles. As the child leaves the last hurdle the teacher/coach nominates a marker for the child to accelerate to
- Work two children opposite one another and place a ball approximately 5 metres from the last hurdle. As the children leave the last hurdle each races to get to the ball before the other

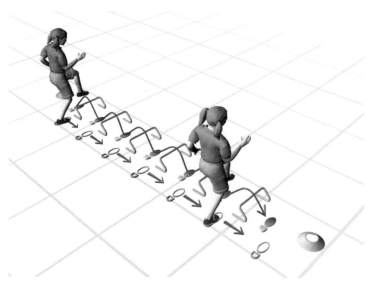

Figure 2.2 Pre-turn

## DRILL | *RUNNING FORM – LEADING LEG RUN*

### Aim
To develop quick, efficient steps and running techniques.

### Area/equipment
Indoor or outdoor area. Using hurdles, marker dots or sticks, place approximately 8 obstacles in a straight line at 2-foot intervals. Place a marker dot 1 metre from each end of the line to mark a start and finish.

### Description
Child runs down the line of obstacles, crossing over each one with the same lead leg. The aim is to just clear the obstacles. Repeat the drill using the opposite leg as the lead.

### Key teaching points
■ The knee-lift should be no more than 45 degrees
■ Use short, sharp steps
■ Maintain strong arm mechanics
■ Maintain an upright posture
■ Stand tall and do not sink into the hips

### Sets and reps
1 set of 4 reps, 2 leading with the left leg and 2 with the right.

### Variations/progressions
■ A good exercise for changing direction after running in a straight line is to place 3 marker dots at the end of the obstacles at different angles 2–3 metres away; on leaving the last obstacle, the child sprints out to the marker dot nominated by the teacher/coach
■ Vary the distance between the hurdles to achieve different stride lengths

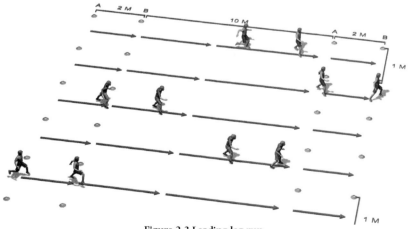

Figure 2.3 Leading leg run

**DRILL**

*RUNNING FORM –*
## QUICK SIDESTEP DEVELOPMENTS

### Aim
To develop correct, precise and controlled lateral stepping movements.

### Area/equipment
Indoor or outdoor area. Place 3 hurdles side by side about 18 inches apart.

### Description
Child stands on the outside of either hurdle 1 or hurdle 3 so that he/she will step over the middle of each hurdle. The child performs lateral mechanics movement while clearing each hurdle – on clearing hurdle 3 he/she repeats the drill in the opposite direction.

### Key teaching points
- Maintain correct lateral running form/mechanics
- Maintain correct arm mechanics
- Do not sink into the hips
- Keep the head up
- Do not lean too far forwards
- Use small steps and work off the balls of the feet
- Do not use an excessively high knee-lift

### Sets and reps
2 sets of 10 reps, 5 to the left and 5 to the right, with 1 minute recovery between sets.

### Variations/progressions
- Work with a teacher/coach, who should randomly direct the child over the marker dots
- Add 2 Macro V Hurdles to add lift variation

## DRILL | RUNNING FORM – SIDESTEP DEVELOPMENT

### Aim
To develop efficient and economical lateral sidesteps.

### Area/equipment
Indoor or outdoor area. Place 8 Micro V Hurdles side on, 1 metre apart and staggered laterally. Position a finish marker dot in the same pattern as the hurdles.

### Description
Child works inside the channel created by the hurdles, and steps over each hurdle with one foot as he/she moves laterally down and across the channel. On reaching the end of the channel, walk back to the start and repeat the drill.

### Key teaching points
■ Bring the knee up 45 degrees over the hurdle
■ Do not overstride across the hurdle
■ Maintain correct arm mechanics/strong arm drive
■ Keep the hips square
■ Do not sink into the hips

### Sets and reps
2 sets of 3 reps, with a walk-back recovery between reps and 2 minutes between sets.

### Variation/progression
Perform the drill backwards.

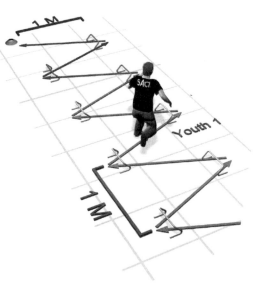

Figure 2.3 Sidestep development

## DRILL | EXERCISE –
### RUNNING FORM – LATERAL STEP

### Aim
To develop efficient and economical lateral steps.

### Area/equipment
Indoor or outdoor area. Using hurdles, marker dots or sticks, place approximately 8 obstacles in a straight line at 2-foot intervals. Place a marker dot 1 metre from each end of the line to mark a start and finish.

### Description
Child steps over each obstacle while moving sideways.

### Key teaching points
- Bring the knee up to just below 45 degrees
- Do not skip sideways – step!
- Push off from the back foot
- Do not pull with the lead foot
- Maintain correct arm mechanics
- Maintain an upright posture
- Keep the hips square
- Do not sink into the hips

### Sets and reps
1 set of 6 reps, 3 leading with left shoulder and 3 with the right.

### Variation/progression
Place several different-coloured markers 2 metres from the last hurdle at different angles. As the child leaves the last hurdle the teacher/coach nominates a marker for the child to accelerate to.

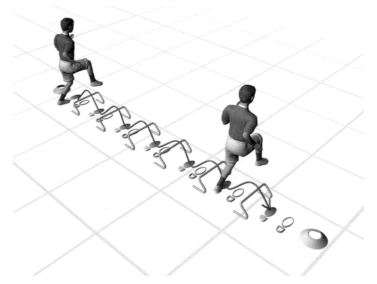

Figure 2.4 Lateral step

## DRILL   *RUNNING FORM – 1-2-3 LIFT*

### Aim
To develop an efficient leg cycle, rhythm, power and foot placement.

### Area/equipment
Indoor or outdoor area 20–25 metres long, marker dots.

### Description
Child moves in a straight line and after every third step the leg is brought up in an explosive action to 90 degrees. Continue the drill over the length prescribed working the same leg and then repeat the drill leading with the other leg. Marker dots can be placed to mark the spot where the leg is brought up explosively.

### Key teaching points
- Keep the hips square
- Work off the balls of the feet
- Try to develop and maintain a rhythm
- Keep eyes and head up and look ahead
- Maintain correct arm mechanics
- Maintain an upright posture

### Sets and reps
1 set of 4 reps, 2 leading with the left leg and 2 with the right.

### Variations/progressions
- Alternate the lead leg during a repetition
- Vary the lift sequence, e.g. 1-2-3-4-lift, etc.

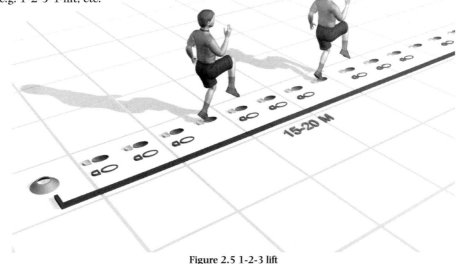

Figure 2.5 1-2-3 lift

## DRILL  JUMPING – SINGLE JUMPS

### Aim
To develop jumping techniques, power, speed and control.

### Area/equipment
Indoor or outdoor area. Ensure the surface is clear of any obstacles. Use 4-, 7- or 12-inch hurdles.

### Description
Child jumps over a single hurdle and on landing walks back to the start point to repeat the drill.

### Key teaching points
■ Maintain good arm mechanics
■ Do not sink into the hips on take-off or landing
■ Land on the balls of the feet
■ Do not fall back on the heels

### Sets and reps
2 sets of 4 reps, with 1 minute recovery between each set.

### Variation/progression
Introduce stability work, child to hold position on landing.

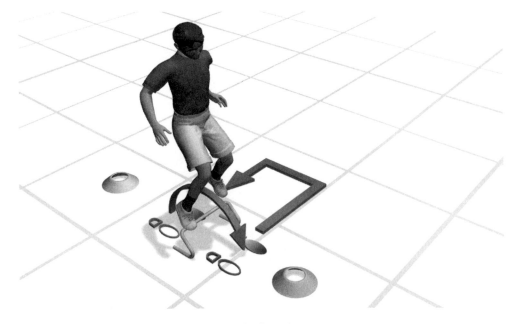

Figure 2.6 Single jumps

# DRILL

*JUMPING –*
## SINGLE JUMPS OVER AND BACK

### Aim
To develop jumping techniques, power, speed and control.

### Area/equipment
Indoor or outdoor area. Ensure the surface is clear of any obstacles.
Marker dots.

### Description
Child jumps over a single hurdle and on landing turns and jumps back
over the hurdle to repeat the drill.

### Key teaching points
- Maintain good arm mechanics
- Do not sink into the hips on take-off or landing
- Land on the balls of the feet
- Do not fall back on the heels

### Sets and reps
2 sets of 4 reps, with 1 minute recovery between each set.

### Variation/progression
Introduce stability work, child to hold position on landing.

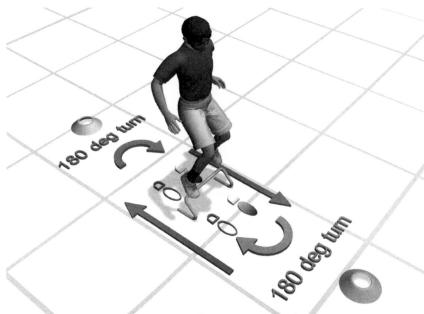

Figure 2.7 Single jumps over and back

## DRILL
### JUMPING –
### SINGLE JUMP WITH 180-DEGREE TWIST

### Aim
To develop jumping techniques, power, speed and control.

### Area/equipment
Indoor or outdoor area. Ensure the surface is clear of any obstacles.
Use 4-, 7- or 12- inch hurdles.

### Description
Child jumps and twists 180 degrees over a single hurdle and on landing walks back to the start point to repeat the drill.

### Key teaching points
- Maintain good arm mechanics
- Do not sink into the hips on take-off or landing
- Land on the balls of the feet
- Do not fall back on the heels

### Sets and reps
2 sets of 4 reps, with 1 minute recovery between each set.

### Variation/progression
Introduce stability work, child to hold position on landing.

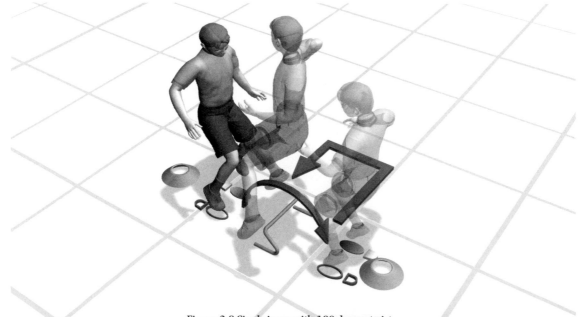

Figure 2.8 Single jump with 180 degree twist

# DRILL — *JUMPING – LATERAL SINGLE JUMPS*

### Aim
To develop jumping techniques, power, speed and control.

### Area/equipment
Indoor or outdoor area. Ensure the surface is clear of any obstacles. Use 4-, 7- or 12-inch hurdles.

### Description
Child jumps laterally over a single hurdle and on landing walks back to the start point to repeat the drill.

### Key teaching points
- Maintain good arm mechanics
- Do not sink into the hips on take-off or landing
- Land on the balls of the feet
- Do not fall back on the heels

### Sets and reps
2 sets of 4 reps, with 1 minute recovery between each set.

### Variations/progressions
- Introduce stability work, hold position on landing
- Child to jump laterally over and back

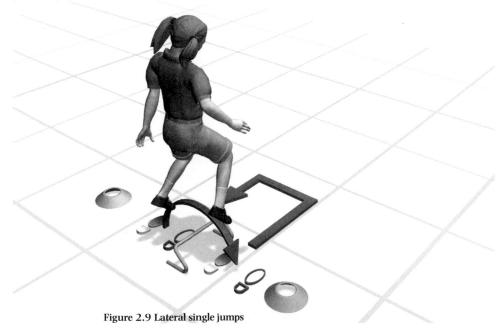

Figure 2.9 Lateral single jumps

## DRILL    FORWARD JUMP – MULTIPLE JUMPS

### Aim
To develop maximum control while taking off and landing. To develop controlled directional power.

### Area/equipment
Indoor or outdoor area. Place 6–8 hurdles of 4, 7 or 12 inches in height at 2-foot intervals in a straight line.

### Description
Child jumps forwards over each hurdle in quick succession until all hurdles have been cleared, then walks back to the start and repeats the drill.

### Key teaching points
- Use quick rhythmic arm mechanics
- Do not sink into the hips at the take-off and landing phases
- Land and take off from the balls of the feet
- Stand tall and look straight ahead
- Maintain control
- Gradually build up the speed

### Sets and reps
2 sets of 6 reps, with 1 minute recovery between each set.

### Variation/progression
Introduce stability work, child to hold position after each jump.

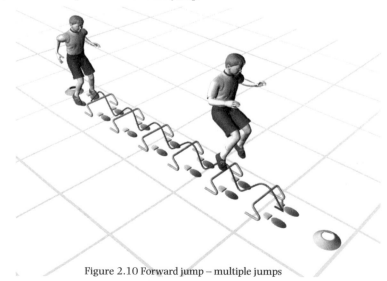

Figure 2.10 Forward jump – multiple jumps

## DRILL   *LATERAL JUMP – MULTIPLE JUMPS*

### Aim
To develop maximum control while taking off and landing. To develop controlled directional power.

### Area/equipment
Indoor or outdoor area. Place 6–8 hurdles of 4, 7 or 12 inches in height at 60 cm intervals in a straight line.

### Description
Child jumps laterally over each hurdle in quick succession until all hurdles have been cleared, then walks back to the start and repeats the drill.

### Key teaching points
- Use quick, rhythmic arm mechanics
- Do not sink into the hips on take-off or landing
- Land and take off from the balls of the feet
- Stand tall and look straight ahead
- Maintain control
- Gradually build up the speed

### Sets and reps
2 sets of 6 reps, with 1 minute recovery between each set.

### Variation/progression
Introduce stability work, child to hold position on landing.

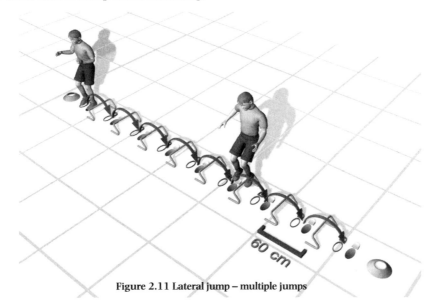

**Figure 2.11 Lateral jump – multiple jumps**

# DRILL  HOP JUMPS – MULTIPLE HOPS

### Aim
To develop maximum control while taking off and landing. To develop controlled directional power.

### Area/equipment
Indoor or outdoor area. Place 6–8 hurdles of 4, 7 or 12 inches in height at 60 cm intervals in a straight line.

### Description
Child hops over each hurdle in quick succession until all hurdles have been cleared, then walks back to the start and repeats the drill.

### Key teaching points
■ Use quick, rhythmic arm mechanics
■ Do not sink into the hips on take-off or landing
■ Land and take off from the balls of the feet
■ Stand tall and look straight ahead
■ Maintain control
■ Gradually build up the speed

### Sets and reps
2 sets of 6 reps, with 1 minute recovery between each set.

### Variations/progressions
■ Alternate landing and take-off foot
■ Introduce stability work, hold position on landing, then repeat.

Figure 2.12 Hop jumps – multiple hops

## *180-DEGREE*
## *TWIST JUMPS – MULTIPLE JUMPS*

### Aim
To develop maximum control while taking off and landing. To develop controlled directional power.

### Area/equipment
Indoor or outdoor area. Place 6–8 hurdles of 4, 7 or 12 inches in height at 60 cm intervals in a straight line.

### Description
Child jumps and twist 180 degrees over each hurdle in quick succession until all hurdles have been cleared, then walks back to the start and repeats the drill.

### Key teaching points
- Use quick, rhythmic arm mechanics
- Do not sink into the hips on take-off and landing
- Land and take off from the balls of the feet
- Stand tall and look straight ahead
- Maintain control
- Gradually build up the speed

### Sets and reps
2 sets of 6 reps, with 1 minute recovery between each set.

### Variations/progressions
- Introduce stability work, hold position on landing
- Introduce alternate twisting over each hurdle

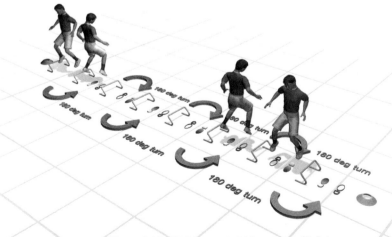

Figure 2.13 - 180 degree twist jumps – multiple jumps

# DRILL    RUNNING FORM –
## STRIDE FREQUENCY AND EFFICIENCY

### Aim
To practise the transfer from the acceleration phase to an increase in stride frequency and length required when running – to develop an efficient leg cycle, rhythm, power and foot placement.

### Area/equipment
Indoor or outdoor area, 20–30 metres long. Place 12 coloured, 4-foot sticks or canes flat on the ground at 5–6 foot intervals (the intervals will be determined by the size and age of the group).

### Description
Starting 10 metres away from the first stick the child accelerates towards the sticks and aims to land just past each one. After the last stick the child gradually decelerates. Return to the start and repeat the drill.

### Key teaching points
- Do not overstride
- Work off the balls of the feet
- Try to develop and maintain a rhythm
- Keep eyes and head up as if looking over a fence
- Maintain correct mechanics
- Maintain an upright posture
- Stay focused
- Alter distances between strides for different ages and heights

### Sets and reps
1 set of 3 reps.

### Variations/progressions
- Set up the stride frequency sticks as shown in Figure 2.14. The sticks now control the acceleration and deceleration phases
- Add change of direction during the deceleration phase
- After deceleration add stability skill by getting the children to stand still for 3–4 seconds on the balls of the feet with their hands out in a defensive position

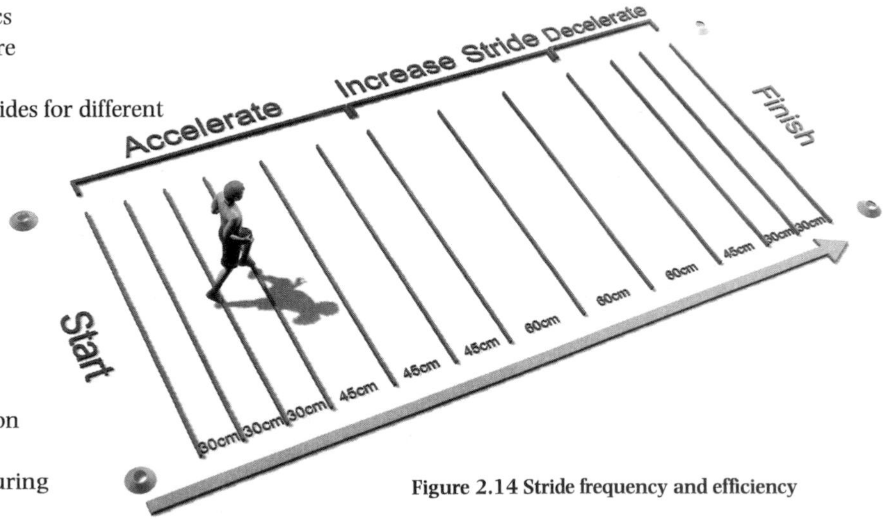

Figure 2.14 Stride frequency and efficiency

# DRILL

## *RUNNING FORM –*
## *HURDLE MIRROR DRILLS*

### Aim
To improve random agility. To challenge the child's ability to mirror another child's movements.

### Area/equipment
Indoor or outdoor area. Mark out a grid with 2 lines of 8 hurdles or marker dots with 2 feet between each hurdle and 2 metres between each line of hurdles.

### Description
Children face each other while performing mechanics drills up and down the lines of hurdles. One child initiates the movements while the partner attempts to mirror them. Children can perform both lateral and linear mirror drills.

### Key teaching points
- Stay focused on your partner
- The child mirroring should try to anticipate the lead child's movements
- Maintain correct arm mechanics

### Sets and reps
Each child performs 3 sets of 30-second work periods. Ensure 30 seconds recovery between each work period.

### Variations/progressions
- First-to-the-marker-dot – as above, except a ball is placed between the 2 lines of hurdles. The proactive partner commences the drill as normal then accelerates to touch the dot. The reactive child attempts to beat the proactive child to the dot
- Lateral drills performed as above – children work in pairs with only 2 hurdles per child, effective for improving short-stepping, lateral skills

**Figure 2.15 Hurdle mirror drills**

# *DRILL* RUNNING FORM – CURVED ANGLE RUN

### Aim
To develop controlled, explosive fast feet while running on a curved angle.

### Area/equipment
Indoor or outdoor area. Place 10 hurdles in a curved formation, 2 feet apart. Place a marker dot at each end, approximately 2 metres from the first and last hurdles respectively.

### Description
Child performs running drill as already described: the Dead-leg run (see p. 81), Lateral stepping or Leading leg run – same leg leading over each hurdle.

### Key teaching points
■ Work both left and right sides
■ The knee-lift should be no more than 45 degrees
■ Use short, sharp steps
■ Maintain powerful arm mechanics
■ Maintain an upright posture
■ Look ahead at all times

### Sets and reps
Each child performs 1 set of 4 reps. Leave 30 seconds recovery between each work rep.

### Variations/progressions
■ Introduce a foam ball
■ Introduce stability, hold position after each step
■ Introduce tighter curves
■ Use immediately after straight run hurdle work

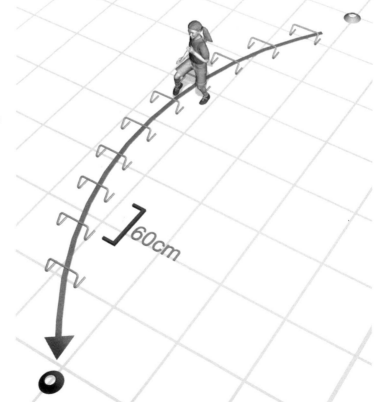

Figure 2.16 Curved angle run

| **DRILL** | *RUNNING FORM –* |
|---|---|
| | *COMBINATION COMPLEX MECHANICS* |

## Aim

To bring together running form drills into different combinations so that children become more comfortable at changing movement patterns when required.

## Area/equipment

Indoor or outdoor area. Place 2 straight lines of 6 or 8 hurdles side by side and 1 metre apart with 2 feet between each hurdle.

## Description

Child performs a mechanics drill down 1 line of hurdles then turns and performs a different drill down the next line of hurdles.

## Key teaching points

- Maintain correct arm mechanics
- Work off the balls of the feet
- Try to develop and maintain a rhythm
- Keep eyes and head up and look ahead
- Maintain an upright posture
- Keep the hips square

## Sets and reps

2 sets of 4 reps.

## Variation/progression

Vary the combination of sets of drills down each line of hurdles

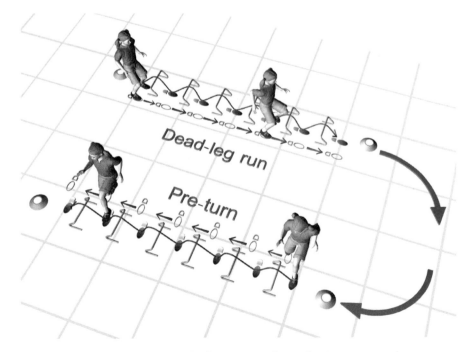

Figure 2.17 Combination complex mechanics

## DRILL
### RUNNING FORM –
### COMPLEX MECHANICS – THE SQUARE

### Aim
To bring together running form drills into different combinations so that children become more comfortable at changing movement patterns when required.

### Area/equipment
Indoor or outdoor area. Place 4 lines of hurdles or marker dots in a square 2 feet apart.

### Description
Child performs a different mechanics drill down each line of hurdles until the square is completed.

### Key teaching points
- Maintain correct arm mechanics
- Work off the balls of the feet
- Try to develop and maintain a rhythm
- Keep eyes and head up and look ahead
- Maintain an upright posture
- Keep the hips square

### Sets and reps
2 sets of 4 reps.

### Variation/progression
Vary the combination of sets of drills down each line of hurdles

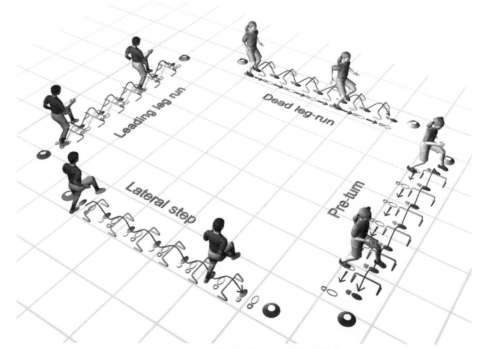

Figure 2.18 Complex mechanics – the square

## DRILL

### *INTEGRATING RUNNING*
# *FORM WITH GAME SKILL DEVELOPMENT*

### Aim
To develop correct, precise and controlled lateral stepping movements while manipulating or striking.

### Area/equipment
Indoor or outdoor area. Place 3 hurdles side by side about 18 inches apart.

### Description
Child stands on the outside of either hurdle 1 or hurdle 3 so that he/she will step over the middle of each hurdle. The child performs lateral movements mechanics while clearing each hurdle – on clearing hurdle 3 he/she repeats the drill in the opposite direction.

### Key teaching points
- Maintain correct lateral running form/mechanics
- Maintain correct arm mechanics
- Do not sink into the hips
- Keep the head up
- Do not lean too far forwards
- Use small steps and work off the balls of the feet
- Do not use an excessively high knee-lift

### Sets and reps
2 sets of 6 reps, 3 to the left and 3 to the right with 60 seconds' recovery between sets.

### Variations/progressions
- Work with a teacher/coach, who should randomly direct the child over the hurdles
- Add 2 Macro V Hurdles to add lift variations
- Work in groups of three: child 1 works through the hurdles, children 2 and 3 stand at either end, throwing and catching the ball to child 1 as he/she reaches their end ( see Figure 2.19)
- After stepping over the last hurdle, child 1 can turn and receive the ball from another child (see Figure 2.20)

Figure 2.19 Form with game skill development

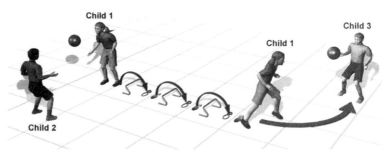

Figure 2.20

## DRILL

## INTEGRATING RUNNING
# FORM WITH LATERAL GAMES SKILLS

### Aim
To develop efficient and economical lateral sidesteps while catching and throwing the ball.

### Area/equipment
Indoor or outdoor area. Place 8 Micro V Hurdles side on, 1 metre apart and staggered laterally. Position a finish marker in the same pattern as the hurdles.

### Description
Child 1 works inside the channel created by the hurdles, stepping over each hurdle with one foot as he/she moves laterally down and across the channel. On stepping on the outside hurdle a ball is thrown for him/her to catch and return by child 2 situated on that side. This action is also repeated on the opposite side with child 3. After receiving the ball children 2 and 3 walk backwards into position ready for the next time child 1 steps over the outside hurdle.

### Key teaching points
■ Bring the knee up 45 degrees over the hurdle
■ Do not overstride across the hurdle
■ Maintain correct arm mechanics/strong arm drive
■ Keep the hips square
■ Do not sink into the hips

### Sets and reps
2 sets of 3 reps, with a walk-back recovery between reps and 2 minutes between sets.

### Variation/progression
Perform the drill backwards.

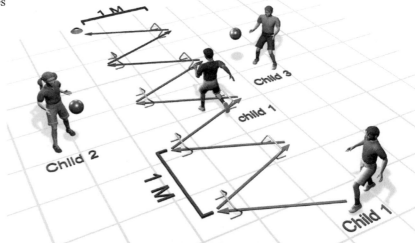

Figure 2.21 Form with lateral games skills

# CHAPTER 3 INNERVATION

## *INCREASING THE SPEED OF MOVEMENT*

Innervation is the transition stage from warm-up and mechanics to periods of work of higher intensity that activate the neural pathways, or in more simple terms, cause the nerves to fire the muscle as quickly as possible. Faster-moving hands, feet and body control enables children to perform co-ordinated movements of speed and agility such as sidesteps, short, explosive sprints, fast hands to catch and the quickness to turn and chase. The key in this section is to quicken the movements without compromising the quality of movement techniques. It is important to perfect the movement slowly then increase the intensity and quickness.

## Health and Safety

- Be aware of spacing of ladders, i.e. create plenty of space at either end and between

- Avoid fatigue, which will lead to poor technique and slow feet

- Improved foot placement helps prevent foot and ankle injuries

- Never secure the ladders to the surface

- Start slowly before getting fast

## Developing and progressing ladder drills

- Vary direction of movement

- Alternate leading foot

- One foot moves quickly whilst the other is used for support

- Vary size of movements, use small inside the ladder, larger ones outside the ladder

- Add twists and turns

- Vary height of movements, both in stepping and jumping

- Change direction in and out of the ladder

- Use marker dots in the squares in the ladder to indicate change of movement or action

- Introduce stops and starts, this will help develop stability

- Incorporate ball skills (manipulation) out of the ladder, progress to ball skills in the ladder

- Children to carry rackets/bats so that striking drills can be introduced in and out of the ladder

## DRILL  FAST FOOT LADDER – SINGLE WALK

### Aim
To develop awareness, confidence and familiarity with technique and equipment.

### Area/equipment
Use an indoor or outdoor area. Use a Fast Foot Ladder – ensure that this is the correct ladder for the type of surface being used.

### Description
Child covers the length of the ladder by placing a foot in each ladder space at a walking pace, and returns to the start by walking back along the outside of the ladder.

### Key teaching points
- Maintain correct form/mechanics
- Ensure elbows are held at 90 degrees and arms are driven forwards and backwards at the correct angle
- Maintain an upright posture
- Encourage walking on the balls of the feet, keeping off the toes
- Stress that quality not quantity is important

### Sets and reps
2 sets of 3 reps, with 30 seconds recovery between each set.

### Variation/progression
Single lateral walk.

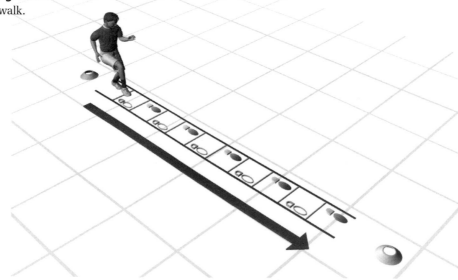

Figure 3.1 Fast Foot Ladder – single walk

## DRILL   *FAST FOOT LADDER – SINGLE RUN*

### Aim
To develop linear fast feet with control, precision and power.

### Area/equipment
Use an indoor or outdoor area. Use a Fast Foot Ladder – ensure that this is the correct ladder for the type of surface being used.

### Description
Child covers the length of the ladder by placing a foot in each ladder space (see Figure 3.2). and returns to the start by jogging back beside the ladder.

### Key teaching points
- Maintain correct running form/mechanics
- Start slowly and gradually increase the speed
- Maintain an upright posture
- Stress that quality not quantity is important

### Sets and reps
2 sets of 3 reps, with 1 minute recovery between each set.

### Variations/progressions
- Child to throw beanbag into one of the ladder squares, run and pick up the beanbag and continue running down the ladder
- Place a marker dot halfway down the ladder, when the child reaches the dot they stop, count to three and start again
- Stability drill: place marker dot halfway down the ladder, when the child reaches the dot they stand on one foot and hold the position, count to five and start again

Figure 3.2 Fast Foot Ladder – single run

## DRILL  FAST FOOT LADDER – SINGLE LATERAL STEPS

### Aim
To develop lateral fast feet with control, precision and power.

### Area/equipment
Use an indoor or outdoor area. Use a Fast Foot Ladder – ensure that this is the correct ladder for the type of surface being used.

### Description
Child covers the length of the ladder moving sideways by placing a foot in each ladder space, and returns to the start by jogging back beside the ladder.

### Key teaching points
■ Maintain correct running form/mechanics
■ Start slowly and gradually increase the speed
■ Maintain an upright posture
■ Stress that quality not quantity is important
■ Push off from the back foot

### Sets and reps
2 sets of 3 reps, with 1 minute recovery between each set.

### Variations/progressions
■ Place a marker dot outside one of the ladder squares; on reaching it the child should step out of and back into the ladder square before continuing down the ladder
■ Manipulation skills: on completing the ladder drill, leave balls at the far end of the ladder; one can be bounced back to the starting point

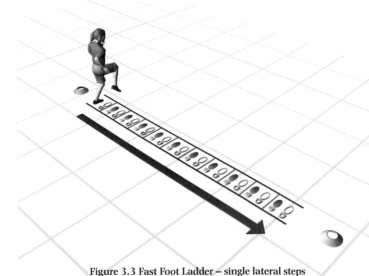

Figure 3.3 Fast Foot Ladder – single lateral steps

## DRILL    *FAST FOOT LADDER – LATERAL STEP IN AND OUT*

### Aim
To develop laterally in-and-out fast feet with control, precision and power.

### Area/equipment
Use an indoor or outdoor area. Use a Fast Foot Ladder – ensure that this is the correct ladder for the type of surface being used.

### Description
Child to cover the length of the ladder by running down the side of the ladder and stepping in and out each ladder space with the nearest leg. This is repeated on the other side.

### Key teaching points
- Maintain correct running form/mechanics
- Start slowly and gradually increase the speed
- Maintain an upright posture
- Head up, and focus on an object on horizon

### Sets and reps
2 sets of 4 reps, with a 1 minute recovery between each set.

### Variations/progressions
- Introduce stepping into every second ladder space
- Randomly place marker spot in ladder space where child has to step in and out

## DRILL | *FAST FOOT LADDER – SMALL DEAD-LEG RUN*

### Aim

To develop quick, short knee-lift and positive foot placement for running.

### Area/equipment

Use an indoor or outdoor area, Fast Foot Ladder – ensure that the correct ladder for the type of surface is being used.

### Description

Child works down the side of the ladder, keeping the outside leg straight in a locked position. The inside leg moves over the ladder rungs in a short, fast cycle motion, while the outside leg swings along just above the ground.

### Key teaching points

■ Maintain correct arm mechanics
■ Maintain an upright posture and strong core
■ Keep the hips square and stand tall
■ Only increase the speed when technique has been mastered
■ Listen for too much sound from foot placement, this means child is hitting the floor with a flat foot

### Sets and reps

2 sets of 4 reps, with a 1 minute recovery between each set.

### Variations/progressions

■ Integrate step in, step out and dead-leg run
■ Randomly place Macro V Hurdle in ladder square for higher knee-lift

# DRILL    *FAST FOOT LADDER – ICKY SHUFFLE*

### Aim
To develop control, balanced lateral movement.

### Area/equipment
Use indoor or outdoor area. Use a Fast Foot Ladder – ensure that this is the correct ladder for the type of surface being used.

### Description
Child covers the length of the ladder performing lateral footwork drill as shown in Figure 3.5

### Key teaching points
- Maintain correct lateral form/mechanics
- Start slowly and gradually increase the speed
- Stress that quality not quantity is important
- Keep off the heels
- Do not let child sink into the hips
- Do not let child skip with both feet in the air

### Sets and reps
2 sets of 3 reps, with 1 minute recovery between each set.

### Variation/progression
Place a marker dot directly outside one of the ladder squares, when the child's outside foot steps on the marker dot the position is held for 3 seconds. This will help develop stability

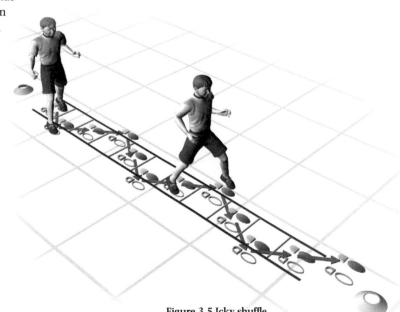

Figure 3.5 Icky shuffle

## DRILL    FAST FOOT LADDER – DOUBLE RUN

### Aim
To develop very fast linear feet with control, precision and power.

### Area/equipment
Indoor or outdoor area. Use a Fast Foot Ladder – ensure that this is the correct ladder for the type of surface being used.

### Description
Child covers the length of the ladder by placing both feet in each ladder space (see Figure 3.6), and returns to the start by jogging back beside the ladder.

### Key teaching points
- Maintain correct running form/mechanics
- Start slowly and gradually increase the speed
- Maintain an upright posture
- Stress that quality not quantity is important

### Sets and reps
2 sets of 3 reps, with 1 minute recovery between each set.

### Variations/progressions
- Child performs drill laterally, putting both feet in each ladder space while moving sideways
- Child throws beanbag into one of the ladder squares, runs and picks it up, then continues running down the ladder
- Place a marker dot halfway down the ladder; the child reaches the dot and stops, counting 3 before starting again
- Stability drill: place marker dot halfway down the ladder, the child reaches the dot, stands on one foot and holds the position, counts to 5 and starts again

Figure 3.6 Double run

## DRILL     *FAST FOOT LADDER – HOPSCOTCH*

### Aim
To develop combined jumping techniques, balance and co-ordination.

### Area/equipment
Use an indoor or outdoor area. Use a Fast Foot Ladder – ensure that this is the correct ladder for the type of surface being used.

### Description
Child covers the length of the ladder by jumping into the first square with feet together, the next with one foot either side of the square, and so on, then returns to the start by jogging back beside the ladder.

### Key teaching points
- Maintain correct jumping form/mechanics
- Start slowly and gradually increase the speed
- Maintain an upright posture
- Stress that quality not quantity is important
- Keep off the heels

### Sets and reps
2 sets of 3 reps, with 1 minute recovery between each set.

### Variations/progressions
- Place a marker dot in one of the squares, where the child stops, counts to 3 and starts again.
- Place a marker dot in one of the squares, where the child repeats the last jump again, i.e. another jump with feet together or a jump with feet across the ladder
- Add stability work: when the child's feet come together he or she lifts one foot, holding the position for 5 seconds

Figure 3.7 Fast Foot Ladder – hopscotch

## DRILL

### FAST FOOT LADDER –
### TWO STEPS FORWARDS AND ONE BACK

### Aim
To develop forward and backward momentum, balance, stability and control.

### Area/equipment
Use an indoor or outdoor area. Use a Fast Foot Ladder – ensure that this is the correct ladder for the type of surface being used.

### Description
Child to take 2 single steps forwards and 1 step backwards, repeating this pattern of movement to the end of the ladder.

### Key teaching points
- Start slowly and build up the speed gradually
- Ensure arms are correctly used
- It is important that arms are not swung across the body, this will throw the child off balance
- Child to stand tall and use strong core
- Arms to be driven while moving forwards and backwards

### Sets and reps
2 sets of 3 reps, with 1 minute recovery between each set.

### Variations/progressions
- Place a marker dot in a ladder square, where the child should step out of then back into the ladder before continuing the drill down the ladder
- Drill can be performed sideways, remember to work both left and right shoulders

Figure 3.8 Two steps forwards and one back

## DRILL FAST FOOT LADDER – SINGLE SPACE JUMPS

### Aim
To develop small, controlled jumps with speed, precision, balance and co-ordination.

### Area/equipment
Use an indoor or outdoor area. Use a Fast Foot Ladder – ensure that this is the correct ladder for the type of surface being used.

### Description
Child covers the length of the ladder by jumping into each ladder space with both feet together, then returns to the start by jogging back beside the ladder.

### Key teaching points
- Maintain correct jumping form/mechanics
- Start slowly and gradually increase the speed
- Ensure that the arms are used in the correct manner to assist the jumps
- Maintain upright posture
- Ensure that on landing the child does not sink too deep at the hips
- Stress that quality not quantity is important

### Sets and reps
2 sets of 3 reps, with 1 minute recovery between each set.

### Variations/progressions
- Child to throw a beanbag into one of the ladder squares, where he/she steps over it and continues to the end of the ladder
- Place 2 or 3 marker dots into different squares, on landing on a dot the child holds the position for 3–4 seconds, then continues down the ladder; this is good for developing stability

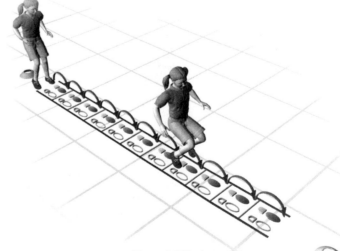

**Figure 3.9 Single space jumps**

## DRILL   FAST FOOT LADDER –
## TWO JUMPS FORWARDS AND ONE BACK

### Aim
To develop forward and backward momentum, balance, stability and control while jumping.

### Area/equipment
Use an indoor or outdoor area. Use a Fast Foot Ladder – ensure that this is the correct ladder for the type of surface being used. NB: An outdoor ladder on a hard surface must not be used for this drill.

### Description
Child takes 2 single jumps forwards, one jump backwards and repeats this pattern of movement to the end of the ladder.

### Key teaching points
- Start slowly and build up the speed gradually
- Land and take off on the balls of the feet
- Ensure arms are correctly used
- It is important that arms are not swung across the body, this will throw the child off balance
- Child to stand tall and use strong core
- Arms to be driven while moving forwards and backwards
- Child should not go so fast as to lose control at the end of the ladder

### Sets and reps
2 sets of 3 reps, with 1 minute recovery between each set.

### Variations/progressions
- Place a marker dot in a ladder square, where the child jumps out of and back into the ladder then recommences the drill
- Drill can be performed sideways – remember to work both left and right shoulders

Figure 3.10 Two jumps forwards and one back

## DRILL **FAST FOOT LADDER – 'TWIST AGAIN'**

### Aim
To develop controlled and balanced hip-twisting rotation skills.

### Area/equipment
Use an indoor or outdoor area. Use a Fast Foot Ladder – ensure that this is the correct ladder for the type of surface being used.

### Description
Child to move down the ladder with feet together in a twisting movement. Feet to be pointing to the left in one ladder square then pointing to the right when they land in the next square.

### Key teaching points
■ Work on the balls of the feet
■ Use arms to help balance
■ Hips to be twisted with control
■ Do not sink into the hips

### Sets and reps
2 sets of 3 reps, with 1 minute recovery between each set.

### Variations/progressions
■ Perform drill sideways down the ladder
■ Place a marker dot in one of the ladder squares, where the child should hold the position for 3 seconds, then continue the drill to the end of the ladder; this will help stability

Figure 3.11 Twist again

# DRILL FAST FOOT LADDER – HOP IN-AND-OUT

## Aim
To develop balance, co-ordination and body control.

## Area/equipment
Use an indoor or outdoor area. Use a Fast Foot Ladder – ensure that this is the correct ladder for the type of surface being used.

## Description
Child hops into the first ladder square, then diagonally out to the side of the next square and then diagonally back into the next ladder square. This sequence is maintained down the ladder. Child to perform drill first on one leg and then on the other.

## Key teaching points
- Work on the balls of the feet
- Use correct arm mechanics for drive, balance and control
- Do not bend at the hips

## Sets and reps
2 sets of 3 reps, with 1 minute recovery between each set.

## Variations/progressions
- Introduce hopping from one side of the ladder into a square then out to the other side of the ladder
- Place a marker dot in one of the ladder squares, where the child holds the position for 3 seconds, then continues the drill to the end of the ladder; this helps stability

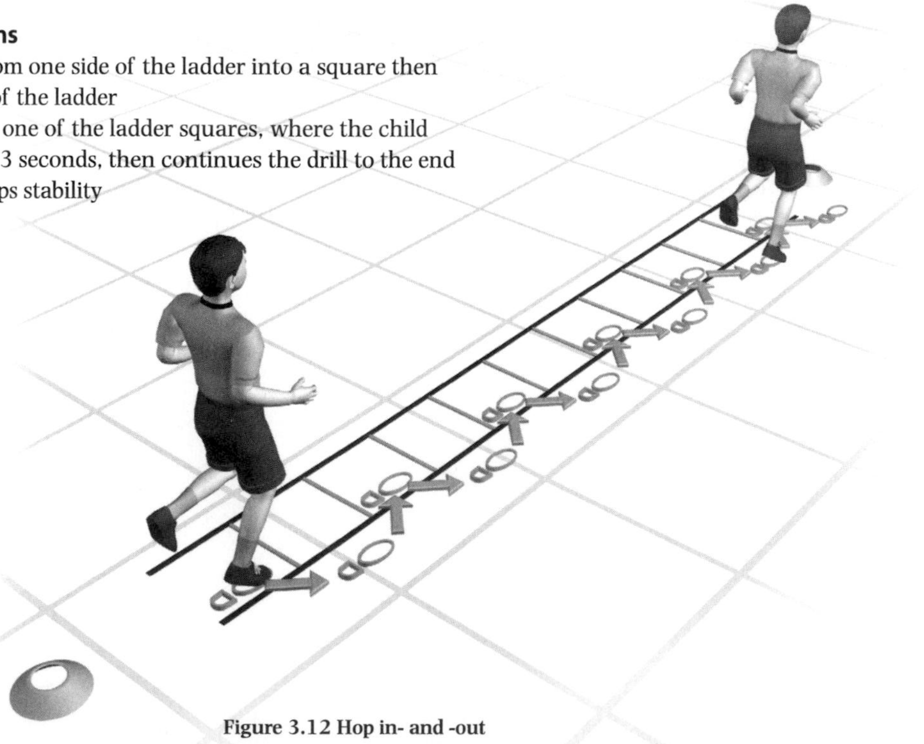

Figure 3.12 Hop in- and -out

# *DRILL* *FAST FOOT LADDER – CARIOCA*

### Aim
To develop hip mobility and speed, balance and control.

### Area/equipment
Use an indoor or outdoor area. Use a Fast Foot Ladder – ensure that this is the correct ladder for the type of surface being used.

### Description
Child to cover the length of the ladder by moving laterally performing the 'Carioca'. The rear foot crosses in front of the body then moves around to the back while, simultaneously, the lead foot does the opposite. The arms also move across the front and back of the body.

### Key teaching points
- Start slowly and build up the tempo
- Work on the balls of the feet
- Keep the shoulders square
- Always perform drill on both sides

### Sets and reps
2 sets of 3 reps, with 1 minute recovery between each set.

### Variation/progression
Perform the drill with 2 ladders placed next to each other so that the children can complete the drill while mirroring each other.

Figure 3.13 Carioca

## DRILL    *SPOTTY DOGS*

### Aim

To improve shoulder and arm speed and activate core muscles. To develop explosive forward and backward stepping movement with co-ordination and balance.

### Area/equipment

Use an indoor or outdoor area. Use a Fast Foot Ladder – ensure that this is the correct ladder for the type of surface being used.

### Description

Child to cover the length of the ladder moving laterally, alternately stepping in and out of the ladder squares, while chopping the legs and arms, left leg to right arm, right leg to left arm. The range of the movement for the arms is from the side of the body up to the side of the face.

### Key teaching points

- Keep on the heels
- Arm action is a chop not a punch
- Land and take off on the balls of the feet
- Maintain upright posture
- Keep the head up

### Sets and reps

2 sets of 3 reps, with 1 minute recovery between each step.

### Variations/progressions

- Child can perform the drill using opposite arms and legs
- Child can perform the drill holding beanbags in each hand
- Child can perform the drill holding a balloon in each hand

Figure 3.14 Spotty dogs

| **DRILL** | *FAST FOOT LADDER – T FORMATION* |
|---|---|

## Aim

To develop linear and lateral change of direction and patterns of movement.

## Area/equipment

Use indoor or outdoor area. Place 2 ladders in a T formation with 3 marker dots placed at the end of each ladder.

## Description

Child accelerates down the ladder using single steps. On reaching the second ladder, the child moves laterally either left or right using short lateral steps. On coming out of the ladder the child turns and runs back to the start.

## Key teaching points

- Maintain correct running form/mechanics
- Use strong arm drive when transferring from linear to lateral steps

## Sets and reps

3 sets of 4 reps, with 1 minute recovery between each set (2 moving to the left and 2 to the right).

## Variations/progressions

- Start with a lateral run and upon reaching the end ladder accelerate in a straight line forwards down the ladder
- Mix and match previous quick feet ladder drills described earlier

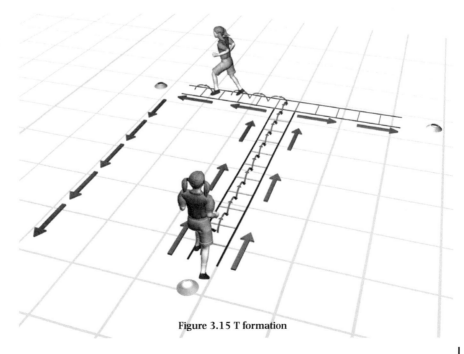

Figure 3.15 T formation

**DRILL** **FAST FOOT LADDER – CROSSOVER**

### Aim
To develop speed, agility and change of direction. To improve child's reaction time, peripheral vision and timing.

### Area/equipment
Use large indoor or outdoor area. Place 4 ladders in a cross formation leaving a clear centre square of about 3 square metres. Place a marker dot 1 metre from the start of each ladder.

### Description
Divide children into four equal groups and locate them at the start of each ladder. Simultaneously the first child from each group accelerates down the ladder performing a single-step drill; on reaching the end of the ladder each child accelerates across the centre square and joins the end of the queue. Do not travel down the opposite ladder.

### Key teaching points
- Maintain correct running form/mechanics
- Keep the head and eyes up and be aware of other children particularly around the centre area

### Sets and reps
3 sets of 6 reps, with 1 minute recovery between each set.

### Variations/progressions
- At the end of the first ladder sidestep to the right or left and join the appropriate adjacent ladder
- Vary the Fast Foot Ladder drills performed down the first ladder
- Include a 360-degree turn in the centre square, this is effective for positional awareness

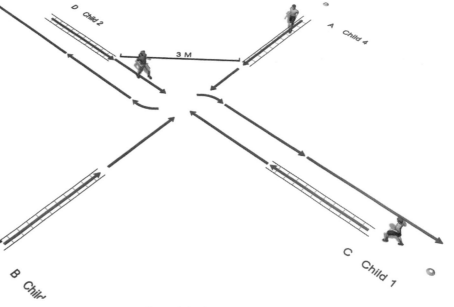

Figure 3.16 Crossover

## DRILL
# *FAST FOOT LADDER –*
# *CROSSOVER HEAD TO HEAD*

### Aim
To develop linear acceleration, change of direction and visual awareness.

### Area/equipment
Use indoor or outdoor area, place 2 ladders in line with a 5 metre gap in the middle. Place a marker spot at the start of each ladder.

### Description
Split children up into two groups and locate them at the start of each ladder. Simultaneously the children accelerate down the ladder towards each other performing single step drill, then, accelerate into the middle space still towards each other. They then swerve and pass each other on the outside and then proceed to join the queue at the start of the opposite ladder. Do not travel down the opposite ladder.

### Key teaching points
- Maintain correct running form/mechanics
- Keep eyes and head up and be aware of other children
- Ensure children are aware of which side to pass each other in the centre area

### Sets and reps
3 sets of 6 reps, with 1 minute recovery between each set.

### Variations/progressions
- Include 360-degree turn as they come out of the ladder
- Introduce a beanbag pass in the middle

# DRILL | *FAST FOOT LADDER –*
# *MIRROR (FOOT STAMP GAME)*

### Aim
To develop explosive footwork and to improve footwork reactions.

### Area/equipment
Use indoor or outdoor area. Use a 15-foot section of ladder.

### Description
Child 1 and child 2 stand opposite each other on either side of the ladder. Starting in the middle, child 1 moves laterally and randomly steps in and out of the ladder. Child 2 responds by mirroring as quickly and accurately as possible the movements of child 1.

### Key teaching points
- Maintain correct lateral running form/mechanics
- Use short, sharp explosive steps
- Work off the balls of the feet
- Use a strong arm drive
- Always keep the hips square

### Sets and reps
3 sets of 2 reps, with a 15-second rest between reps and 2 minutes' recovery between each set. NB: In one set each child should take the lead for 45 seconds.

### Variation/progression
Introduce slight upper body, game-like contact.

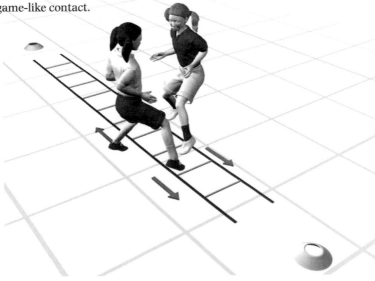

Figure 3.17 Mirror (Foot stamp game)

# CHAPTER 4 ACCUMULATION OF POTENTIAL

## COMBINING QUALITY AND QUICKNESS OF MOVEMENT

When children play, exercise and compete in sport a whole range of movements occur which include hand–eye and foot co-ordination, body and visual awareness. Manipulation skills such as throwing and catching can also be present. An example is a simple game of tag; children will accelerate, decelerate, sidestep, dodge, jump and even step backwards to avoid being caught. These movements happen in a random sequence and will occur over a varying period of time. It is here that the full range of Speed, Agility and Quickness can be observed.

Up to this point we have looked at numerous Dynamic Flex™, Mechanics and Innervation drills and practices in isolation. This part of the Junior Continuum begins to bring these drills together to combine movements. This is vital for good development because, of course, when children are physically active in play or sport, movements are clustered not isolated.

Programmed agility circuits are an incredibly effective way of combining movements in a controlled environment. Over a period of time as the children become more competent we can also incorporate manipulation skills such as throwing and catching. These in turn will place greater demands on hand–eye and foot co-ordination and work towards developing an all-round athlete.

There also exists a golden opportunity to create an environment that promotes Health Related Fitness and conditioning activity with children.

This section may also be used by the teacher/coach to evaluate a child's progress in a structured way.

## Health and safety

■ Lay out circuits carefully with respect to spacing

■ Monitor fatigue levels, allowing appropriate rest periods

■ If Agility Discs are used there must be no running, jumping or sliding onto/off discs

# DRILL | *BALANCE AND AGILITY*

### Aim
To develop balance, proprioception and stability.

### Area/equipment
Use an indoor or outdoor area and an Agility Disc.

### Description
Child to stand and balance with both feet on the Agility Disc.

### Key teaching points
- Keep strong core
- Do not sink into the hips
- Use arms to help maintain balance
- Keep head still

### Sets and reps
1 set of 5 reps of 45 seconds, with 15 seconds' recovery.

### Variations/progressions
- Get-ups: child starts in a low position on the Agility Disc, stands up to finish on one leg
- Receive a ball pass and volley the ball back
- Stop a rolling ball
- Catch a passed ball
- Bend and touch a nominated marker spot

## DRILL　*SEATED BALANCE AND AGILITY*

### Aim
To develop core proprioception, balance and stability.

### Area/equipment
Use an indoor or outdoor area and an Agility Disc.

### Description
Child sits on an Agility Disc, keeping as upright as possible. Legs are held out slightly bent. First, one foot is raised off the ground and then when that is mastered, both feet are raised off the ground together and held for the allocated time.

### Key teaching points
- Always start with one foot off the ground first
- Keep head still and up
- Use arms to maintain balance

### Sets and reps
1 set of 5 reps of 45 seconds, with 15 seconds' recovery

### Variations/progressions
- Raise 2 feet up
- Pairs sit back to back, passing the ball around
- 'Simon says' arm movements game

# DRILL    SWERVE DEVELOPMENT RUNS

### Aim
To develop fine-angled swerve running, balance, co-ordination and body control.

### Area/equipment
Use a large indoor or outdoor area. Place 8–12 poles, cones or marker spots in a zigzag formation. The distance between them should be 1 to 2 metres at varying angles (this will make the runs more realistic). The total length of the run will be 15–20 metres.

### Description
The child accelerates from the first cone and swerves from inside the channel turning from cone to cone, then gently jogs back to the starting cone before repeating the drill.

### Key teaching points
■ Maintain correct running form/mechanics
■ Work on shortening the steps used in the turn
■ Focus on increasing the speed of the arm drive when coming out of the turns
■ Do not take wide angles around the cones
■ Keep the head and eyes up

### Sets and reps
2 sets of 3 reps, with 30 seconds' recovery between each rep and 1 minute recovery between each set.

### Variation/progression
Go around the cones.

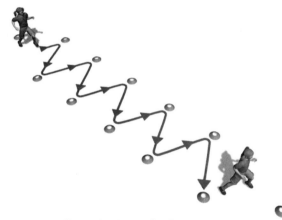

Figure 4.1 Swerve development runs

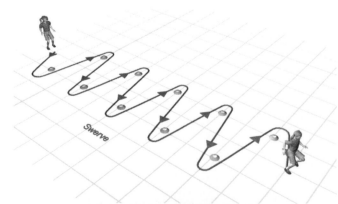

Figure 4.2 Swerve development runs cont...

| **DRILL** | **FAST FEET ZIGZAG RUNS** |

### Aim

To develop acceleration, transfer from linear to lateral zigzag movement back to linear movement with control, balance and precision.

### Area/equipment

Use an indoor or outdoor area, mark out a grid using 2 ladders and 10 to 12 cones or poles, place ladder first then the cones or poles in a zigzag formation finally finishing off with a ladder at the end (see Fig. 4.3).

### Description

Child runs down the ladder to develop acceleration; on coming out of the ladder the child moves sideways to the first cone and repeats this movement up to the last cone. On the last cones the child straightens up and runs down the final ladder, then walks back to the start and repeats the drill.

### Key teaching points

- Maintain correct running form/mechanics
- Keep the hips facing the direction of running
- Use short steps
- Do not skip
- Use good arm mechanics

NB: Arm mechanics are as vital in lateral movements as they are in linear movements; many children forget to use their arms when they are moving sideways.

### Sets and reps

2 sets of 3 reps, with a walk-back recovery between each rep and 1 minute recovery between each set.

### Variations/progressions

- Vary the drills on the ladder
- Up-and-back – enter the grid sideways and move forwards to the first cone then backwards to the next

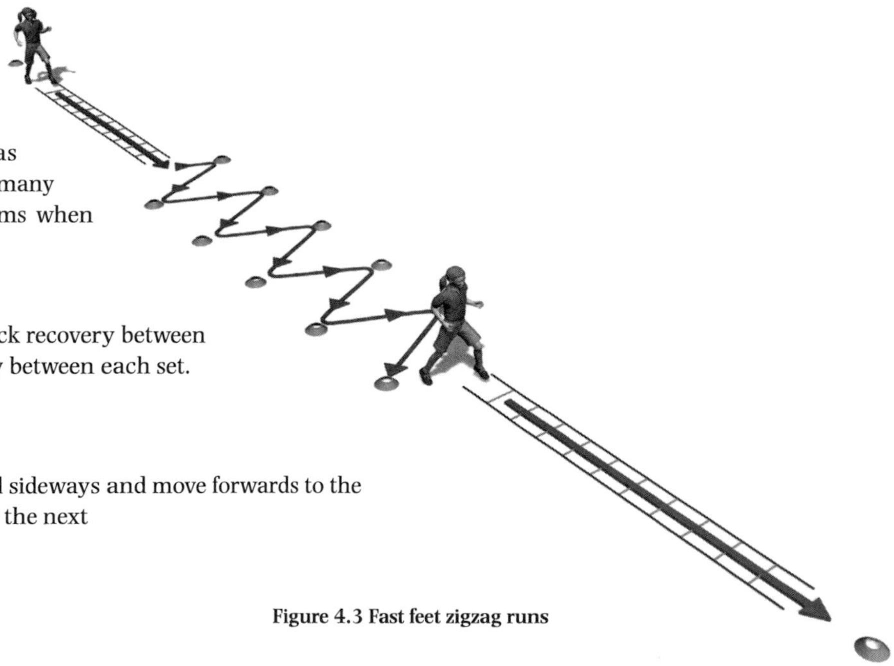

Figure 4.3 Fast feet zigzag runs

# DRILL  FOUR TURN, FOUR ANGLE RUN

## Aim
To develop turns and angled change of direction with control, balance and co-ordination.

## Area/equipment
Use indoor or outdoor area, using 5 marker dots/cones or poles placed in a cross formation with a centre cone. The points of the cross are 5 metres from the centre and equally spaced out from the centre.

## Key teaching point
Ensure correct movement mechanics are maintained.

## Description
Child starts on the centre cone E, and runs around cone A and back to the centre cone E, changes angle of the run to move out towards and around cone B and then back to the centre cone E. Continue this for cones C and D.

## Sets and reps
2 sets of 2 reps, with 1 minute recovery between each set and 2 minutes between each rep.

## Variation/progression
Add 2 or 3 additional cones between centre cone E and cones B and D. Here the child swerves in between the cones, out and back.

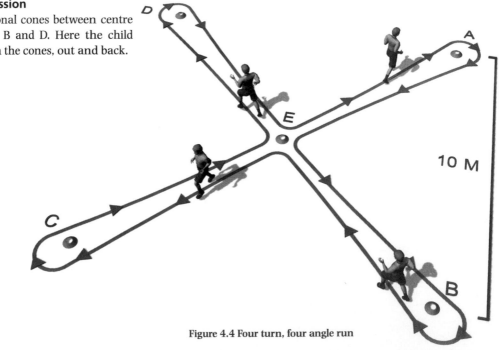

Figure 4.4 Four turn, four angle run

## DRILL  COMBINATION RUNS

### Aim
To develop combination of running and movement patterns that will help develop gross motor skills of the child.

### Area/equipment
Indoor or outdoor area, depending on space available. Place hurdles, Fast Foot Ladder, poles/cones/marker dots in different formations and combinations.

### Description
Child to complete circuit performing the different drills, i.e. stepping, jumping, swerving etc.

### Key teaching points
Maintain correct running form/mechanics for all activities.

### Sets and reps
2 sets of 2 reps, with a 1 minute recovery between each set and 2 minutes' recovery between each rep.

### Variations/progressions
- Vary the drills at hurdles, ladders etc
- Set out identical circuits, introduce team relays

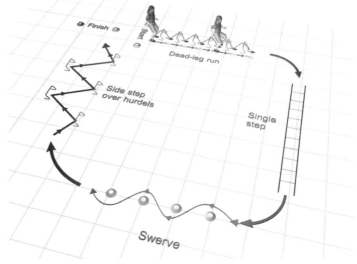

Figure 4.5

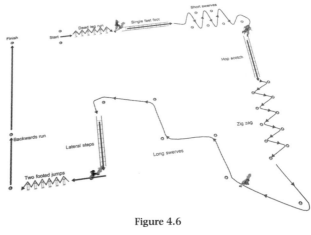

Figure 4.6

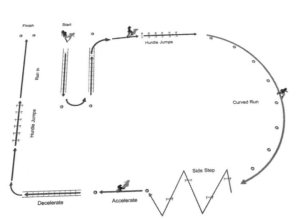

Figure 4.7

# DRILL  TEAM COMBINATION RUNS

## Aim

To develop multidirectional movement, balance, co-ordination and body control while competing against another team.

## Area/equipment

Use a large indoor or outdoor area. Place 2 sets of identical hurdles, Fast Foot Ladders, poles/cones/marker dots in different formations and combinations next to each other. Ensure there is a starting and finishing point for the teams.

## Description

Teams to complete circuit performing the different drills, i.e. stepping, jumping, swerving etc, while competing against the other team. The team that finishes first or has least mistakes is the winner.

## Key teaching points

- Maintain correct running form /mechanics for all activities
- Ensure that speed is not sacrificed for quality of movement

## Sets and reps

2 sets of 2 reps with 1 minute recovery between each set and 2 minutes' recovery between each rep.

## Variations/progressions

- Vary the drills at hurdles, ladders etc.
- Set out identical circuits, introduce team relays

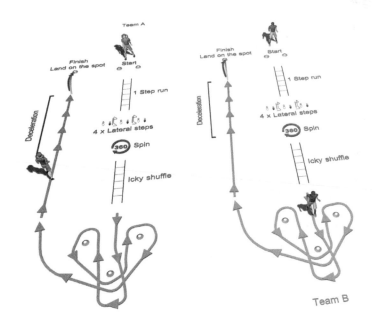

Figure 4.8 Team Combination runs

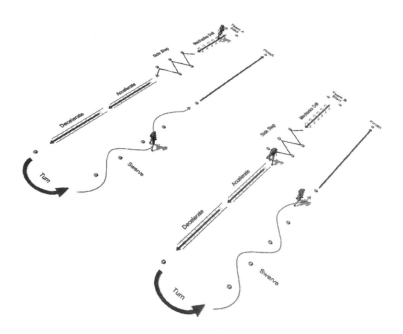

Figure 4.9 Team Combination runs

## DRILL   HEALTH RELATED FITNESS CIRCUITS

### Aim

To improve general health and fitness including cardiovascular, balance, agility, co-ordination, reactions, manipulation and visual skills; to be challenged and have fun at the same time.

### Area/equipment

Use an indoor or outdoor area with marker spots, hurdles, ladders, mats, Agility Discs and Jelly Balls or tennis balls or beanbags. Equipment to be set out into stations so that different drills can be performed.

### Description

Children to perform drills at each station for an allocated time, then move to the next station in the circuit to perform the next drill.

### Key teaching points

- Use the correct techniques required for each station, i.e. correct arm mechanics, posture etc.
- Ensure that all drills are demonstrated prior to warming up
- Provide constant feedback to all children during circuit

### Sets and reps

1 circuit, 40 seconds per station with a 25-second changeover.

### Variation/progression

Add different drills at each station

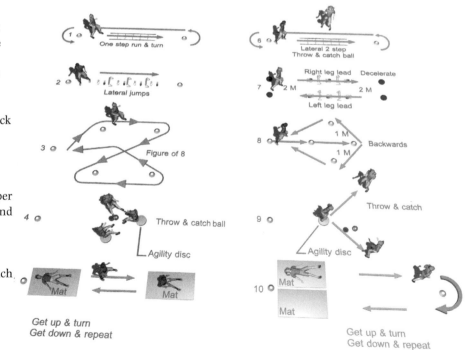

Figure 4.10 Health related fitness circuits

# CHAPTER 5 EXPLOSION

## *IMPROVING THE CONTROL AND QUICKNESS OF RESPONSE*

All children have the ability to improve response times and develop multidirectional explosive movements. While helping children to understand, for example, that getting to the ball or space first is essential in games play, it is possible to develop their ability to move explosively both in a horizontal and vertical direction.

'Let go' drills and 'get-ups' all develop the ability of children to be more explosive. The most crucial element of using these types of drills is the implementation of the contrast phase. This simply means performing a drill without resistance, for one or two repetitions, directly after performing them with resistance. An example of this is running with a Sonic Chute twice over 20 metres and then running again without.

The key is to ensure that quality not quantity is the priority and efforts must be carefully monitored. This is a time for fast action, not exhausting, tongue-hanging-out responses and fatigue.

## Health and Safety

■ Monitor quantities of effort

■ Create clear working grids to avoid collisions

■ Always follow lesson application guidelines and any equipment instructions

■ Allow for plenty of 'run out space' i.e. not too close to walls

# DRILL  VISION AND REACTION – FAST HAND GAMES

### Aim
To develop lightning-quick hand–eye reactions; to be fun and challenging.

### Area/equipment
Indoor or outdoor area. No equipment required.

### Description
Work in pairs. Child 1 puts his/her hands together and holds them slightly away in front of the chest. Child 2 stands directly in front with hands held at the side. The drill begins with child 2 attempting to slap child 1's hands. Child 1 tries to prevent child 2 by moving the hands away as quickly as possible. Children alternate.

### Key teaching points
■ Stand in athletic position
■ Keep head still

### Sets and reps
30 seconds each per drill.

### Variations/progressions
■ Child 1 holds his/her hands out with the palms facing the ground, with tips of thumbs just touching. Child 2 holds hands just above. The drill commences with child 2 attempting to slap both hands before child 1 can react by moving them away
■ Child 1 stands directly in front of child 2, 1–2 metres apart. Child 1 jabs a punch at child 2 who attempts to clap both hands over the fist

## *DRILL*  *VISION AND REACTION – REACTION BALL*

### Aim
To develop lightning-quick hand–eye reactions.

### Area/equipment
Outdoor or indoor area but not a grass surface. Use a Reaction Ball or a tennis/foam ball or beanbag.

### Description
Work in pairs or small groups; standing 5 metres apart. The ball/beanbag is thrown so that it lands in front of the child; because of its structure the ball will bounce in any direction. The child has to react and catch it before it bounces for a second time.

### Key teaching points
- The child catching the ball should work off the balls of the feet and in a slightly crouched position with the hands out ready
- The ball/beanbag should not be thrown hard – it will do the necessary work itself

### Sets and reps
2 sets of 20 reps, with no recovery between each rep and 1 minute recovery between each set.

### Variations/progressions
- Work individually or in pairs by throwing the ball/beanbag against the wall
- Stand on Agility Discs while throwing the ball/beanbag to each other

## DRILL    *GET-UPS*

### Aim
To develop multidirectional explosive acceleration. To improve a child's ability to get up and accelerate all in one movement.

### Area/equipment
Indoor or outdoor area of 10 square metres.

### Description
Child sits on the floor, facing the direction he/she is going to run in with his/her legs straight out in front. On the signal from the teacher/coach, the child gets up as quickly as possible, accelerates for 5 metres and then slows down before jogging gently back to the start position.

### Key teaching points
- Try to complete the drill in one smooth action
- Use correct running form/mechanics
- Do not stop between getting up and starting to run
- Get into an upright position and drive the arms as soon as possible
- Ensure the initial steps are short and powerful
- Do not overstride

### Sets and reps
2 sets of 4 reps, with a jog-back recovery between each rep and 2 minutes' recovery between each set.

### Variations/progressions
- Backward get-ups
- Sideways get-ups
- Lying get-ups from the front, back, left and right
- Kneeling get-ups
- Work in pairs and have get-up competitions chasing a ball
- Work in pairs with one child in front of the other and perform 'tag' get-ups

# DRILL  CHAIR GET-UPS

### Aim
To develop explosive power for acceleration linearly and laterally.

### Area/equipment
Indoor or outdoor area with plenty of room for deceleration – place a chair/stool and 5 markers as shown in Figure 5.1.

### Description
Child sits on a chair and on the teacher/coach's signal will get up and move to the nominated marker dot/cone as quickly as possible. On reaching the marker dot or cone the child should decelerate and walk back to the start position.

### Key teaching points
- Use an explosive arm drive when getting up
- Get into a correct running posture as quickly as possible
- Initial steps should be short and powerful
- Work off the balls of the feet

### Sets and reps
2 sets of 6 reps, with a walk-back recovery between each rep and 2 minutes' recovery between each set.

### Variation/progression
Introduce a 1:2 passing drill at the cones/marker dots.

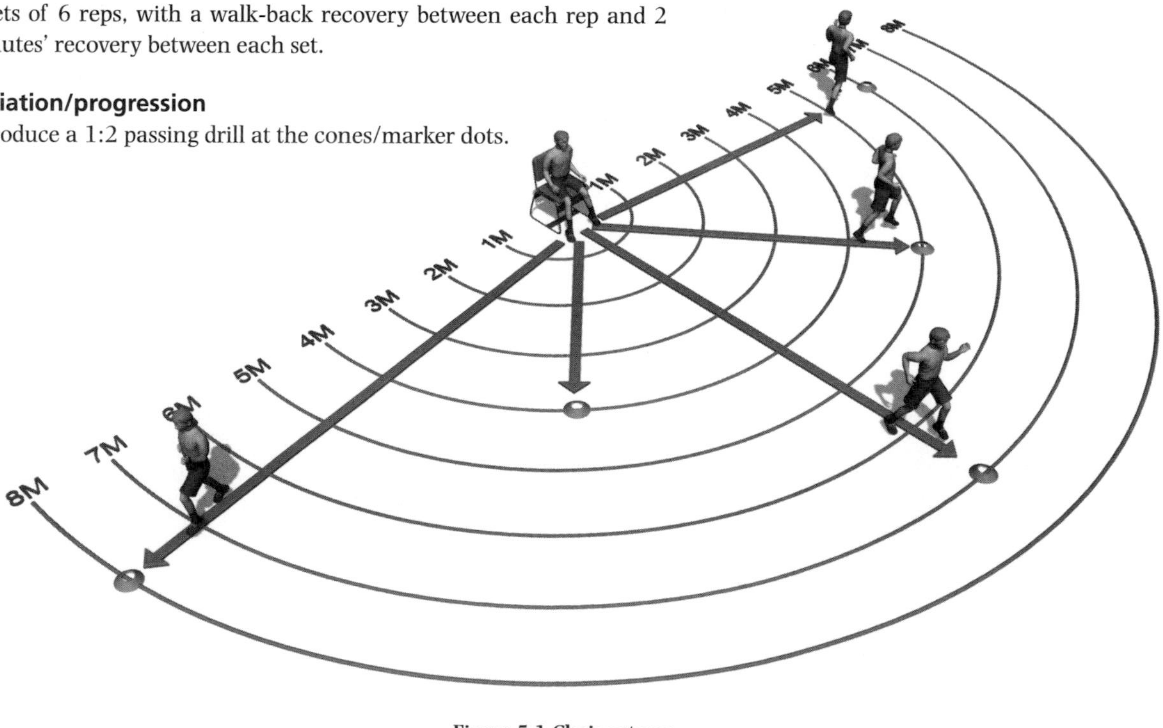

Figure 5.1 Chair get-ups

# DRILL   *LET-GOES*

### Aim
To develop multidirectional explosive acceleration.

### Area/equipment
Indoor or outdoor area of 10 square metres; ensure there is plenty of room for safe deceleration. NB: Strong clothing is preferred; if children are wearing lightweight clothing then a towel can be used.

### Description
Working in pairs, child 1 stands directly in front of his/her partner, child 2, and grips his/her shorts or shirt on both sides. Child 1 tries to accelerate away from child 2, who resists the movement for a few seconds before releasing child 1. Child 1 accelerates away for 2–4 metres before decelerating and walking back to the start position.

### Key teaching points
- Work off the balls of the feet
- Use short steps during the explosion and acceleration phases
- Use good arm drive
- Keep head up
- Child 1 should adopt good running form/mechanics as soon as possible.

### Sets and reps
2 sets of 3 reps, with a walk-back recovery between each rep and 2 minutes' recovery between each set.

### Variations/progressions
- Lateral let-goes
- Backward let-goes
- Let-goes with an acceleration onto a stationary ball
- Let-goes with an acceleration onto a moving ball

## DRILL   *PARACHUTE RUNNING*

### Aim
To develop explosive running over longer distances (sprint endurance) and explosive acceleration.

### Area/equipment
Indoor or outdoor area, 4 marker dots and a parachute. Mark out a grid of 25 metres in length, place one marker dot down as a start marker, and 3 further marker dots at distances of 15 metres, 20 metres and 25 metres from the start marker.

### Description
Wearing the parachute, child accelerates to the 20-metre marker dot then decelerates.

### Key teaching points
■ Maintain correct running form/mechanics
■ Do not worry if the wind and the resistance cause you to feel as though you are being pulled from side to side; this will in fact improve your balance and co-ordination
■ Do not lean into the run too much
■ Quality not quantity is vital

### Sets and reps
2 sets of 4 reps plus 1 contrast run, with a walk-back recovery between each rep and 3 minutes' recovery between each set.

### Variations/progressions
■ Explosive reacceleration – the parachutes have a release mechanism; the child accelerates to the 15-metre marker dot where the child releases the parachute and explodes to the 20-metre marker dot before decelerating
■ Random change of direction – the teacher/coach stands behind the 15-metre marker dot; as the child releases the parachute the teacher/coach indicates a change in the direction of the run; when mastered, the teacher/coach can then introduce the ball for child to run on to during the explosive phase

# DRILL | BALL DROPS

### Aim
To develop explosive reactions.

### Area/equipment
Indoor or outdoor area; 1 or 2 foam balls

### Description
Work in pairs; one child drops the ball at various distances and angles from his or her partner. The ball is dropped from shoulder-height and immediately the partner explodes forwards and attempts to catch the ball before the second bounce. (Distances between children will differ because the height of the bounce will vary depending on the ground surface.)

### Key teaching points
- Work off the balls of the feet, particularly prior to the drop
- Use a very explosive arm drive
- The initial steps should be short, fast and explosive
- At the take-off do not jump, dither or hesitate
- Work on developing a smooth one-movement run

### Sets and reps
3 sets of 8 reps, with 2 minutes' recovery between each set.

### Variations/progressions
- Child to hold 2 balls and to drop just 1
- Work in groups of three with two of the children at different angles alternately dropping a ball for the third child to catch; on achieving this, the child turns and accelerates away to catch/dive on the second ball
- Alter the start positions, e.g. sideways, backwards with a call, seated, etc.

# CHAPTER 6 EXPRESSION OF POTENTIAL

## *PRACTICAL APPLICATION OF ALL MOVEMENT SKILLS*

This stage is short in duration, but very important. The children will experience all the elements of the Junior Continuum into a fun play and even competitive situation. Short tag-type games and random agility tests work really well here. The key is to use all the movement skills that have been practised and improved through the Junior Continuum in real play situations. This stage also provides the opportunity to excite and challenge the children. Most importantly it will guarantee an exhilarating finish to a lesson, so as to ensure that the children will be looking forward to the next one!

Because many of the possible activities can replicate the 'chaos' of games play, they provide another excellent opportunity for the teacher or coach to evaluate how the child is moving once they have to concentrate on tactics and strategies at the same time.

## Health and safety

- Check movement directions and spacing

- Create clearly marked playing areas

# DRILL  CIRCLE BALL

## Aim
To practise using explosive evasion skills.

## Area/equipment
Outdoor or indoor area. Children make a circle about 15 metres in diameter (depending on the size of the group). Foam balls/beanbags.

## Description
One or two children stand in the centre of the circle while the children on the outside have 1 or 2 foam balls. The object is for those on the outside to try and make contact (with the ball) with those on the inside. The children on the inside try to dodge the balls. The winners are the pair who have the least number of hits during their time in the centre.

## Key teaching point
Children on the inside should use the correct mechanics.

## Sets and reps
Each pair to stay in the centre area for 45 seconds.

## Variation/progression
Children in the middle have to hold on to each other's hand or use a Break-Away Belt.

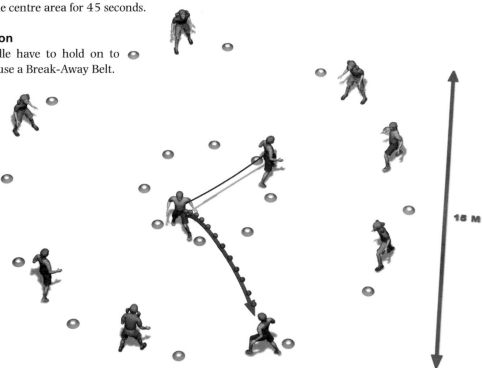

**Figure 6.1 Circle ball**

# DRILL    ROBBING THE NEST

### Aim
To practise multidirectional explosive speed, agility and quickness.

### Area/equipment
Outdoor or indoor area of about 22 square metres, with a centre circle, measuring 2 metres in diameter, marked out with markers. Place a number of foam balls/beanbags/tennis balls in the centre circle.

### Description
Two nominated children defend the 'nest' of the tennis balls with the rest of the children standing on the outside of the square area. The game starts when the outside children run in and try to steal the balls from the nest and run to the outside of the square-safe zone. The two defenders of the nest try to prevent the robbers from getting the balls to the safe zone by tagging them or getting in their way. For every successful tag and prevention, the ball is returned to the centre circle.

### Key teaching points
■ Correct mechanics must be used at all times
■ Children should dodge, swerve, weave, sidestep, etc.
■ Light contact only should be used
■ Keep head up, practise visual awareness at all times

### Sets and reps
Each pair to defend for about 45 seconds.

### Variation/progression
Attackers work in pairs, one attempt to retrieve the foam balls/beanbags/tennis balls from the middle by getting to the ball and rolling it out for the outer partner to field.

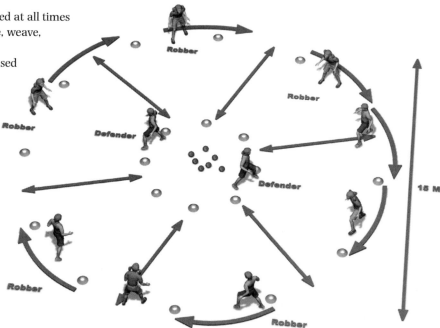

Figure 6.2 Robbing the nest

## DRILL ODD ONE OUT

### Aim
To practise speed, agility and quickness in a competitive environment.

### Area/equipment
Outdoor or indoor area; markers and cricket balls. Mark out a circle of 20–25 metres in diameter and a centre of about 2 metres in diameter.

### Description
Place a number of foam balls/beanbags/tennis balls in the centre area, one fewer than the number of children present. The children are situated on the outside of the larger circle. On the teacher's/coach's call the children start running round the larger circle. On the teacher's/coach's second call they collect a ball from the centre circle as quickly as possible. The child without the ball is the odd one out and performs an activity as directed by the teacher/coach while the next round is completed. The teacher/coach then removes another foam ball/beanbag/tennis ball and repeats the process.

### Key teaching points
- Correct mechanics must be used at all times
- Children should be aware of other children around them.

### Sets and reps
Play the game until a winner emerges.

### Variation/progression
Work in pairs joined together by holding hands or using the Break-Away Belt, one ball between two children. If they break away from each other, they are disqualified.

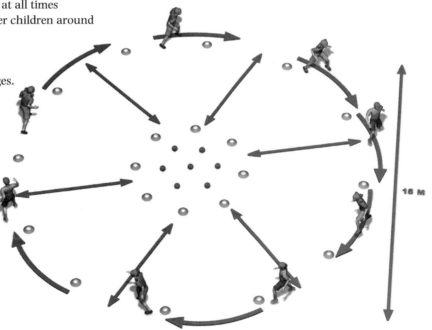

18 M

Figure 6.3 Odd one out

# DRILL  *MARKER TURNS*

### Aim
To practise multidirectional speed, agility and quickness.

### Area/equipment
Outdoor or indoor area of about 20 square metres; 50 small markers.
Place the markers in and around the grid; 25 of the markers should be
turned upside down.

### Description
Working in two small teams (2–3 children), one team attempts to turn
over the upright markers and the other team attempts to turn over the
upside-down markers. The winners are the team that has the largest
number of markers their way up after 60 seconds.

### Key teaching points
- Initiate good arm drive after turning a marker
- Use correct multidirectional mechanics
- Be aware of other children around the area

### Sets and reps
A game should last for 60 seconds.

### Variation/progression
Use 4 teams and allocate 4 different-coloured markers.

# DRILL   *TRUCKS AND TRAILERS*

### Aim
To practise multidirectional speed, agility and quickness of reactions while mirroring another child's movements.

### Area/equipment
Large outdoor or indoor area.

### Description
Working in pairs, one child leads (is the truck) while the other child follows just behind (is the trailer). The child in front moves in different angles and directions while the child behind mirrors the exact movements. The roles are reversed after the recommended period of time.

### Key teaching points
■ Initiate good arm drive after turning a marker
■ Use correct multidirectional mechanics
■ Be aware of other children around the area
■ Maintain a safe distance between the children working together

### Sets and reps
A game should last for 60 seconds and then be reversed.

### Variation/progression
Work in groups of 3 or 4.

**Figure 6.4 Trucks and trailers**

# DRILL THE SNAKE GAME

### Aim
To practise multidirectional speed, agility and quickness, co-ordination, balance and reactions while playing in a team environment.

### Area/equipment
Use an indoor or outdoor area.

### Description
The game starts off with two children holding hands, while the other children spread around the designated area. The object is for the first two children to chase and tag other children, without breaking hands. When tagged the children join hands with the chasers therefore making a 'snake'. The game is finished when the final person is tagged.

### Key teaching points
■ Head up, keeping aware of all other children around
■ Use short steps when changing direction
■ Children who are being chased should use correct form of mechanics for movement

### Sets and reps
Play the game for 4–5 minutes depending on the size of the group.

### Variation/progression
Have two snakes working together.

Figure 6.5 The snake game

# DRILL  THE CONE GAME

## Aim
To develop multidirectional patterns of movement, utilise visual awareness in a team game.

## Area/equipment
Use an indoor or outdoor grid using 4 coloured marker spots, 4 x 3 sets of cones the same colour as the marker spots. The 4 marker spots are placed in a 5-metre square. The 3 cones of the same colour are placed at a marker spot of a different colour.

## Description
Four children are placed, one at each marker spot; the object of the game is for the child to move their 3 coloured cones to their corresponding coloured marker spot. The winner is the child who clears all the cones from their marker spot first.

## Key teaching points
■ Correct mechanics to be used at all times
■ Children should be encouraged to use sidesteps, dodges, swerves etc.
■ Ensure children keep heads up and are aware of the other children

## Sets and reps
Play 1 game until the winner is decided.

## Variation/progression
Increase marker spots and cones to 5–6 stations.

Figure 6.6 The cone game

# DRILL  *BRITISH BULLDOG*

### Aim

To practise multidirectional explosive movements in a pressured situation.

### Area/equipment

Outdoor or indoor area of approximately 20 square metres and about 20 markers to mark out start and finish lines.

### Description

One child is nominated and stands in the centre of the grid, while the rest stand to one side. On the teacher's/coach's call all the children attempt to get to the opposite side of the square without being caught by the child in the middle. When the child in the middle captures another child, she or he joins them in the middle and helps to capture more 'prisoners' (see Fig. 6.7).

### Key teaching points

■ Use correct mechanics at all times
■ Keep head and eyes up to avoid collisions with other children

### Sets and reps

Play British Bulldog for approximately 3–4 minutes before moving on to the more technical aspects of the game.

### Variations/progressions

■ The child in the middle uses a foam ball to touch other children in order to capture them; the ball can be held or thrown
■ 2 children linked by a Break-Away Belt stand in the middle and act as catchers. If the belt breaks apart while touching a runner the touch does not count (see Fig 6.8)

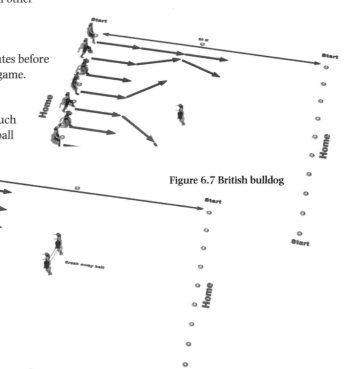

Figure 6.7 British bulldog

Figure 6.8 British bulldog

# CHAPTER 7 VISUAL AWARENESS

The usual eye test is concerned with Static Visual Acuity, i.e. the ability to identify a certain size of letter/number on an eye chart. This is not the only visual ability that a child needs to have in relation to sports performance. There are a number of categories that can be used to ascertain how a child uses vision in the performance of sports skills.

## Static
Seeing static objects clearly, e.g. side-line signals and score boards is desirable but not the most important.

## Dynamic
Maintaining the clarity of an object in motion is vital to the timing of skills, depth and object variations.

## Contrast
Distinguishing the brightness and colour of an object against its background is a key to the performance of, for example, batting skills.

## Colour
Spotting team-mates and following a moving object require good colour recognition.

## Eye movement
Shifting the eyes from place to place rapidly and accurately is important to take in all the factors of a game at a glance.

## Accommodation
Rapidly changing focus will affect the clarity of objects as they move around in space.

## Binocularity
Working the eyes together can affect all judgements of spatial orientation, e.g. following an incoming ball or person.

## Depth perception
The need to judge distances and relationships to objects or places in space is vital in all activities.

## Reaction time
Making sense of and responding to stimuli quickly is increasingly important.

## Central/peripheral
Being aware of that which is to the sides, at the same time as looking at what is central is a prerequisite for children to excel at games.

## Eye–hand–body co-ordination
Integrating the eyes and the hands/body as a unit is important at all levels of performance. Erratic and inconsistent movements will result if there are deficits in this ability.

## Visual adjustability
Rapid adjustment to changing surroundings and environment is necessary to meet the demands of, for example, playing in 'away' venues.

## Visualisation
Mentally rehearsing situations and actions can promote good performance.

Visual awareness can be developed within and at all stages of the SAQ Junior Continuum. Areas such as visual acuity, peripheral vision, tracking and depth perception can be included in many of the drills.

One simple method is to make use of the Visual Acuity Ring and the Peripheral Vision Stick.

# DRILL | *VISUAL AWARENESS – FOLLOW THE THUMB*

### Aim
To develop all-round and peripheral vision.

### Area/equipment
Indoor or outdoor area, standing or seated.

### Description
With either hand, hold arm out in front and make a 'thumbs up' sign. Keeping your head still and only moving your eyes, move the thumb up, down and around making sure you are moving to the extremes of your range of vision. Start slowly and increase the speed of the movement.

### Key teaching point
■ Sit upright with a good posture
■ Try exercise with both left and right hands

### Sets and reps
Continue for 3 minutes in total.

### Variation/progression
Practise drill in different lights, i.e. semi-dark to very bright.

| DRILL | *VISUAL AWARENESS – VISUAL ACUITY RING* |

### Aim
To develop visual acuity, tracking and manipulation skills in catching moving objects.

### Area/equipment
Indoor or outdoor area and a Visual Acuity Ring.

### Description
Work in pairs approximately 5 metres apart. The ring is tossed between the children so that it rotates through the air and is caught on the ball of the colour nominated by the thrower or teacher/coach.

NB: Don't spin the ring too fast at the start as a child may shy away from it instead of catching it.

### Key teaching points
- Keep the head still
- Move the eyes to track the ring
- Work on the balls of the feet so that movement and adjustment can be made quickly
- Hands should be held out in front of the body ready to catch the ring

### Sets and reps
2 sets of 10 reps, with 1 minute recovery.

### Variations/progressions
- Increase the spin gradually
- Vary the receiver's starting position, i.e. sideways, or facing away so the child has to turn and catch
- Receiver catches one- or two-handed
- Ring is thrown horizontally
- Child throws ring up and selects coloured ball to catch it him- or herself
- Spin the ring on the edge, i.e. like spinning a coin; catch the selected ball before the ring hits the ground

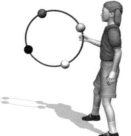

Figure 7.1 Visual acuity ring

## DRILL · VISUAL AWARENESS – NUMBERS AND LETTERS

### Aim
To develop the ability to make subtle focus changes.

### Area/equipment
Indoor or outdoor area, seated or standing; ball or beanbag.

### Description
Draw numbers and letters all over the surface of a ball or beanbag. Toss it from hand to hand, back and forth, reading and calling out as many numbers and letters as possible each time.

### Key teaching point
- Toss the ball/beanbag at steady pace
- Increase speed as you improve

### Sets and reps
Each set lasts for 1 minute. Do 3 sets with 1 minute recovery between each set.

### Variation/progression
Practise drill in different lights, i.e. semi-dark to very bright.

Figure 7.2 Numbers and letters

# DRILL | *VISUAL AWARENESS – PERIPHERAL AWARENESS*

## Aim
To develop peripheral awareness; to help the child detect and react to the ball coming from behind and from the side more quickly.

## Area/equipment
Outdoor or indoor area; use a Peripheral Vision Stick.

## Description
Work in pairs with child 1 behind child 2 who stands in a ready position. Child 1 holds the stick and moves it from behind child 2 into his/her field of vision. As soon as child 2 detects the stick he/she claps both hands over the ball at the end of the stick.

## Key teaching point
- Child 2 should work off the balls of the feet and in a slightly crouched position with the hands held out ready
- Child 1 must be careful not to touch any part of child 2's body with the stick
- Child 1 should vary the speed at which the stick is brought into child 2's field of vision

## Sets and reps
2 sets of 20 reps, with no recovery between each rep and 1 minute recovery between each set.

## Variations/progressions
- Instead of using a Vision Stick, throw balls from behind child 2 who has to fend them off
- A feeder at the back of the performer pushes stick forwards from side to side
- Performer turns and claps ball
- Performer claps ball fed from rear, turns to clap ball now fed from the front
- Three feeders, one on either side feeding in a ball to be caught, alternated with stick holder feeding in from behind for stick to be clapped
- With the ball fed from behind and the head facing forwards, glance the ball with the head as soon as it enters the peripheral vision
- Side 'fends', child pushing stick away with outside of one hand
- Repeat drills standing on one leg to enhance proprioception
- Child randomly receives stick end then ball end of Vision Stick
- Place a hand onto shoulder before ball is lowered onto shoulder; move hand to opposite shoulder
- Increase speed of feeds by having 2 sticks and feeders

**Figure 7.3 Peripheral awareness**

After intense activity children should be given time to reduce gradually the heart rate to near resting, and prepare for the next period of activity again. Warming-down and recovering properly will help to:

- Disperse lactic acid

- Prevent blood pooling

- Return the body's systems to normal levels

- Assist recovery

The structure of the warm-down will reflect the Dynamic Flex™ warm-up movements and static stretches. It need last only a few minutes, depending on the time available. It begins with moderate Dynamic Flex™ movements, which gradually become less intense and energetic. Throughout these exercises there should still be a focus on quality of movement and awareness of balance and general control of the body.

With the inclusion of a series of static stretches, it can be a time when flexibility is explored and children are returned to a relaxed state.

## Health and safety

- Encourage slow, controlled movements

- Emphasise care when moving backwards

## DRILL    HIGH KNEE-LIFT SKIP

Follow the instructions on page 23.

**Aim**
To warm down the hips and buttocks gradually.

**Sets and reps**
2 x 10 metres, 1 forwards and 1 backwards

**Intensity**
60 per cent for the first 10 metres and 50 per cent for the second 10 metres.

## DRILL    WIDE SKIP

Follow the instructions on page 18.

**Aim**
To warm down the hips and ankles.

**Sets and reps**
1 x 10 metres, 1 forwards and 1 backwards.

**Intensity**
40 per cent for the first 5 metres and 30 per cent for the second 5 metres.

## DRILL    KNEE-ACROSS SKIP

Follow the instructions on page 25.

**Aim**
To warm down the hip flexors gradually by lowering the intensity
of the exercise.

**Sets and reps**
2 x 10 metres, 1 forwards and 1 backwards.

**Intensity**
50 per cent for the first 10 metres and 40 per cent for the second 10 metres.

## DRILL    CARIOCA

Follow the instructions on page 29.

**Aim**
To warm down the hips and the core.

**Sets and reps**
2 x 22 metres, 1 leading with left leg and 1 with right.

**Intensity**
30 per cent for the first 10 metres and 20 per cent for the second 10 metres.

## DRILL    SMALL SKIPS

Follow the instructions on page 16.

**Aim**
To warm down the muscles of the lower leg and the ankle.

**Sets and reps**
2 x 10 metres.

**Intensity**
20 per cent for the first 10 metres and 10 per cent for the second 10 metres.

## DRILL    ANKLE FLICKS

Follow the instructions on page 14.

**Aim**
To bring the heart rate down and to stretch the calf and the ankle.

**Sets and reps**
2 x 10 metres, 1 forwards and 1 backwards.

**Intensity**
10 per cent for the first 10 metres and then walking flicks for the second 10 metres.

## DRILL  HURDLE WALK

Follow the instructions on page 35.

### Aim
To bring the heart rate down.

### Sets and reps
2 x 10 metres, 1 forwards and 1 backwards.

### Intensity
Walking.

## DRILL  *WALKING HAMSTRING*

Follow the instructions on page 38.

### Aim
To stretch the backs of the thighs.

### Sets and reps
2 x  10 metres, 1 forwards and 1 backwards.

### Intensity
Walking.

## DRILL  *LATISSIMUS DORSI STRETCH*

### Aim
To stretch the muscles of the back.

### Description
Stand in an upright position and link the hands together in front of the chest. Then push the hands out, simultaneously arching the back forwards.

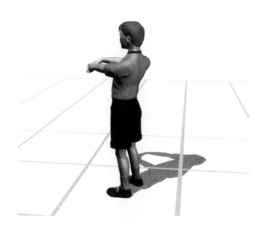

### Key teaching points
- Do not force the arms out too far
- Focus on slow controlled breathing

### Sets and reps
Hold the stretch for about 10 seconds.

# DRILL  *QUADRICEPS STRETCH*

### Aim
To stretch and assist the recovery of the thigh muscles.

### Description
Stand on one leg and bring the other heel in towards the buttock. Using the hand on that side hold the instep of that foot and squeeze it into the buttock. Repeat on the opposite leg.

### Key teaching points
- Keep the knees together
- Ensure the support leg is slightly bent
- Press the hip forwards
- Focus on slow, controlled breathing
- Do not force the stretch, just squeeze it in gently

### Sets and reps
Hold the stretch for about 10 seconds on each leg.

### Variation
The exercise can be performed while the child is lying down on his/her side on the floor.

# DRILL  *HAMSTRING STRETCH*

### Aim
To stretch and assist the recovery of the hamstring.

### Description
Work in pairs. One child raises a leg at a 90-degree angle. The partner holds the back of the heel. The toe of the raised leg is pulled towards the shin (dorsiflex) and kept straight as the partner gently raises the leg.

### Key teaching points
- Focus on slow, controlled breathing
- Bend forwards from the hip, do not lean back
- The partner is to assist by raising the leg gently – do not force the stretch

### Sets and reps
Hold the stretch for about 10 seconds on each leg.

**DRILL** *ADDUCTORS STRETCH*

### Aim
To stretch and assist the recovery of the adductor muscles.

### Description
Stand with the legs apart, bend one knee and keep the foot at a 45-degree angle. The other leg should be straight. Repeat on the opposite leg.

### Key teaching points
- Focus on slow, controlled breathing
- Do not force the stretch
- Keep the back straight
- Do not allow the knee of the bent leg to go beyond the toes

### Sets and reps
Hold the stretch for about 10 seconds on each leg.

**DRILL** *CALF STRETCH*

### Aim
To stretch and assist the recovery of the calf muscles.

### Description
Stand with the legs split and both feet pointing forwards, one leg to the front and other to the back. The weight should be transferred to the forward knee and then gently back. Repeat with other leg.

### Key teaching points
- The front knee should not move further than over the ankle
- The back leg should be kept straight – it is this calf that will be stretched
- Focus on slow, controlled breathing
- Do not force the stretch
- Apply the weight slowly to the front foot

### Sets and reps
Hold the stretch for about 10 seconds on each leg.

# CHAPTER 9

# IMPLEMENTING THE SAQ JUNIOR PROGRAMME

## DEVELOPING SKILFUL MOVEMENT

As previously stated, there is tremendous flexibility in how this programme may be used to improve all elements of a child's movement.

It will be helpful when structuring units of work for the school situation or training programmes for sports performers to consider how children best learn. Skill Learning is best taught by progressing from simple to complex skills and from general to specific skills, e.g. perform a good 'Dead Leg' movement (see p. 92 ) before attempting the more complicated 'Icky' Shuffle (see p. 93 ) and establish good movement mechanics in the ladders before including a throw-and-catch routine.

Allow children to learn by first seeing a clear demonstration of the activity and being given simple instructions on what they should do. If they are able to explore the new skills, they discover what they can already do and can experiment with the new movement challenges, e.g. moving sideways along a ladder may be performed adequately with feet going into the spaces but with the child's hips twisted. The new focus is to try and keep the hips parallel with the black band of the ladder.

This movement can then be combined with, for example, catching a ball at the end of the ladder. The activity can be put into context by application to a 2 v 2 game situation where, for example, the child moves sideways behind one of the defenders to find a space to receive a pass. This puts the performer in a situation where he or she learns to select appropriate movements and apply them to the game. With sufficient practice, lateral movement using effective push off the trailing foot and quick lateral steps with fast arms is consolidated and refined. Adaptation and extension of the movement vocabulary takes place when the child then decides to dodge sideways the 'other way' with a feint before losing the defender to receive a pass with added time and space. (See QCA Schemes of Work for Physical Education.)

Another example of this process is given in the Appendix, p. 154.

Once a range of skills has been selected and practised by children moving through the process just outlined, it may useful for the teacher/coach to reflect on the performance by considering the 'Building Bricks Guide' below. This will allow movements to be made easier or harder depending on the level of success achieved by the performers.

## 'Building Bricks' Guide

Activities and practices can be modified using the following practice framework, which is particularly useful during the EXPLORATORY phase of learning and to challenge pupils further once a skill has been mastered.

### Quality
(What you want to see in every movement!)

| How | Where | | | |
|---|---|---|---|---|
| **Speed** | **Efficiency** | **Direction** | **Level** | **Position** |
| fast | light (like a?) | on the spot | tall | own space |
| slow | heavy | forwards | short | on |
| go faster (accelerate) | smooth | backwards | high | over |
| go slower (decelerate) | jerky | sideways | low | under |
| slow motion | softly | left/right | up | behind |
| fast/slow (erratic) | noisily | diagonal | down | in front |
| sustained | with spring | zig zag | | between |
| stopping | with rhythm | straight line | | around |
| | with/without arms | curve | | beside |
| | explode | pattern | | in and out |
| | | twist | | together |
| | | turn | | at the same time |

To assist younger children it may be useful to prompt their movements by suggesting:

Try to move........ like................ Find different ways to .....................
See if you can............................... Show me how to ................

(Adapted from David L. Gallahue *Movement Concepts*.)

## PLANNING A PROGRAMME

To organise the inclusion of SAQ Training into a scheme of work or a year's sports training programme, several approaches may be considered; integration into existing sessions, following the SAQ Continuum and creating SAQ sessions, and building SAQ activities around the development of fundamental manipulation skills are just some possibilities.

Because SAQ Training may be seen as a 'tool' to enhance teaching and coaching that is already in place, it is easy to integrate into an existing programme using the following guidelines and example lesson plans shown in the appendix (see p. 154). NB: Teaching/Coaching points will be found in previous pages.

Regardless of which of the suggested approaches is used, it may be worthwhile to consider beginning children's SAQ work with an introductory session. It is important that children are helped to understand why they are doing SAQ activities and how and where these exercises will contribute to their athletic movement. The aim would be to get children to explore what contributes to 'good movement', by asking questions:

Q – Why does one child appear to move more quickly than another?
A – Because she runs on 'light' feet.
Q – What makes the feet go faster?
A – Fast arms.

This can be done during a simple tag game such as 'Stick in the Mud'. Another option in athletics would be to have children observe their peers in short races. Why is Brian the fastest? Tracie does not win but looks a better runner – why? Once some of the questions have been discussed children can be introduced to improving their movement by using mechanics.

| INTRODUCTORY SESSION LESSON PLAN | |
|---|---|
| **AREA OF ACTIVITY** | **Games or Athletics: Fundamental movement** |
| **TOPIC** | Introduction to running |
| **KEY STAGE 1–2** | |
| **LESSON AIM** | To develop understanding of what is involved in 'good athletic movement'. |
| **LESSON OBJECTIVE** | To introduce pupils to correct running actions. |
| **Warm-up** | Dynamic Flex™ (5 min) 2 lines of children moving forwards and backwards, performing jogs, skips, laterals, lunges, walking hamstring, selection of short sprints. |
| **Game** | Stick in the Mud (5 min). |
| **Mechanics** | To move on the balls of the feet. Hurdles (5 min) – position lines of 3 hurdles; perform Dead Leg, Leading Leg Run, Stride. |
| **Game** | Repeat 'Stick in the Mud' (5 min) with the focus being on how the feet are working. Indoors ask children to 'listen' to their feet. Quick light movement ensures no noise! |
| **Mechanics** | (5 min) Introduce correct arm action and repeat the above drills. |
| **Game** | Repeat the game (5 min) with the focus on improved and faster arm action. To maintain interest, change the rules. |
| **Warm-down** | (5 min) Slow Dynamic Flex™ movements repeated, followed by static stretches. |

## Key questions:

- What is the best part of the foot to run on?
- What is the best way of using the arms?
- If the arms go fast what happens to the feet?

- Is it best to take small or large steps?
- Why is good balance important?
- What role does the head play in movements?

# Integration into existing sessions

An integrated approach allows existing schemes of work or training programmes simply to be modified with all skill development being underpinned by SAQ foundations.

## 8 LESSON DEVELOPMENT

1. Dynamic Flex, Mechanics, Skills, Game (Expression), Warm-down (WD)

2. Dynamic Flex, Mechanics, Skills, Game, WD

3. Dynamic Flex, Fast Feet, Skills, Game, WD

4. Dynamic Flex, Fast Feet, Skills, Game, WD

5. Dynamic Flex, Fast Feet, Skills, Game, WD

6. Dynamic Flex, Accumulation, Skills, Explosion, Game, WD

7. Dynamic Flex, Explosion, Skills, Game, WD

8. Dynamic Flex, Explosion, Skills, Game, WD

This progression can be illustrated below in Fig.10.1.

## APPLICATION IN A UNIT OF WORK

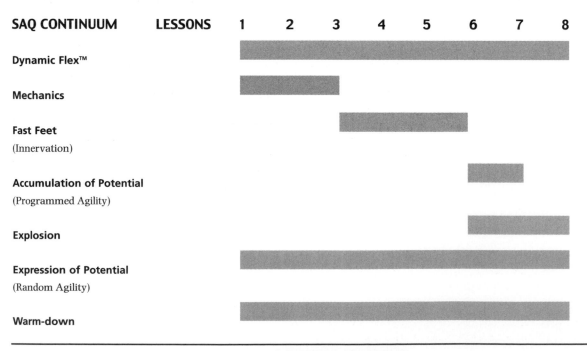

Figure 10.1. SAQ SCHOOLS PROGRAMME

| SAMPLE INTEGRATION LESSON PLAN: Week 6 | |
|---|---|
| **AREA OF ACTIVITY** | **Games: Multidirectional Movement Development** |
| **TOPIC** | Introduction to Programmed Agility and Explosive starts |
| **KEY STAGE 2** | |
| **LESSON AIM** | To develop the ability to change direction with speed and precision. To evaluate the progress of children. |
| **LESSON OBJECTIVE** | To improve patterns of movement and acceleration. |
| **Warm-up** | Dynamic Flex™ (5 min) 2 lines of children moving forwards and backwards, performing jogs, skips, laterals, lunges, hamstring walks, selection of short sprints including 'get-ups'. |
| **Accumulation** | (15 min)  Set up Team Circuit (see p.  ). Allow children to 'have a go'. Encourage them to observe performance, particularly when the speed of each run is increased (if appropriate set up some races). NB: Good mechanics will quickly disappear! |
| **Skills** | (10 min) e.g. shooting a netball, basketball or football. NB: To have a chance to shoot, the player must have successfully outwitted an opponent to keep possession, continue with the dribble or find space so as to receive the pass. This requires multidirectional movement patterns. |
| **Practice** | Children move forwards, sideways and in zigzags before making a shot. |
| **Explosion** | (5 min) In pairs introduce 'Let-Goes'. NB: This can be introduced separately during the next lesson if lesson time is restricted. |
| **Expression** | (Game – 10 min) Encourage elusive running and explosive acceleration through gaps. |
| **Warm-down** | (5 min) Slow Dynamic Flex™ movements repeated + static stretches. |

## FOLLOWING SAQ CONTINUUM LESSONS

The SAQ Continuum can be used in its entirety to provide the structure to session planning where the focus is on developing sound movement principles as a foundation to activity-specific work to follow. This allows good movement to be constantly emphasised in all subsequent work. It can be used to lay down all the basic movement principles at the start of a year, the beginning of a key stage, and has been successfully used in Sports Colleges as part of a Transition Curriculum for years 6 to 7.

## 6 LESSON DEVELOPMENT

### LINEAR movement

1. Dynamic Flex, GAME (context), Mechanics, GAME, Warm-down (WD)

### LINEAR movement

2. Dynamic Flex, Mechanics, Fast Feet, Game, WD

### LINEAR movement

3. Dynamic Flex, Mechanics, Fast Feet, Game, WD

### LATERAL movement

4. Dynamic Flex, Mechanics, Fast Feet,Game, WD

### Decelerate; Accelerate; Programmed Agility

5. Dynamic Flex, Accumulation of Potential Circuit, Game, WD

### EXPLOSION

6. Dynamic Flex, Fast Feet, Explosion, Game, WD

| SAMPLE CONTINUUM LESSON PLAN: Week 4 | |
|---|---|
| **AREA OF ACTIVITY** | **Games: Multidirectional Movement Development** |
| **TOPIC** | Introduction to Lateral Movement |
| **KEY STAGE 1** | |
| **LESSON AIM** | To develop the ability to move sideways with balance and control; to improve the ability to dodge in a simple game. |
| **LESSON OBJECTIVE** | To improve patterns of movement and acceleration. |
| **Warm-up** | Dynamic Flex (5 min) Children moving forwards, backwards and sideways from own marker spot performing basic movements. |
| **Mechanics** | (10 min) Introductory activity – practice side stepping pushing off between 2 spots or between 2 lines. Perform 2 hurdles lateral step. Progress to 3 hurdles. |
| **Innervation** | (Fast Feet) (10 mins) Use short Fast Foot Ladders – lateral steps, repeat in and out, lateral dead leg, mirror work. |
| **Expression (Game)** | (10 mins) Trucks and Trailers (follow my leader running), repeat with 2 trucks. |
| **Warm-down** | (5 mins) Slow Dynamic Flex™ movements repeated, then static stretches. |

# DEVELOPING MANIPULATION SKILLS USING SAQ

Another possible approach with the aim of providing a focus on the development of a wide range of fundamental movement skills is to use the SAQ Continuum in the following way:

## 6 LESSON DEVELOPMENT

**Throw – Catch**
1. Dynamic Flex, SKILLS + Mechanics, Game, WD

**Throw – Catch**
2. Dynamic Flex, SKILLS + Mechanics, Game, WD

**Passing – Feet**
3. Dynamic Flex, SKILLS, Fast Feet, Game, WD

**Dribbling – Bounce**
4. Dynamic Flex, SKILLS, Fast Feet, Game, WD

**Shooting – Hand**
5. Dynamic Flex, Short Circuits to develop positioning for shooting, Game, WD

**Shooting – Feet**
6. Dynamic Flex, Short Circuits to develop positioning for shooting, Game, WD

| SAMPLE MANIPULATION SKILL DEVELOPMENT LESSON PLAN: Week 4 | |
|---|---|
| **AREA OF ACTIVITY** | **Games: Develop co-ordination** |
| **TOPIC** | Bouncing/dribbling a ball |
| **KEY STAGE 1. YEAR 2** | |
| **LESSON AIM** | To develop the ability to control a bouncing ball while moving. |
| **LESSON OBJECTIVE** | To develop the co-ordination necessary to bounce a ball whilst stationary and while moving (dribbling). |
| **Warm-up** | Dynamic Flex (5 min) Children moving forwards, backwards and sideways from own marker spot performing basic movements. Incorporate movements of wrists, pushing-down arm movements. |
| **Skills** | (10 min) Bounce practice using first 2 then 1 hand. Bounce ball on top of marker spot X times, then repeat, moving position of spot to either side of body. Once ball is being pushed downwards and not slapped marker spot can be removed and movement introduced. |

| | |
|---|---|
| **Innervation (Fast Feet)** | (10 mins) Use Long Fast Foot Ladders – linear dead leg, leading leg run, repeat stepping out to touch with foot, marker spots placed at sides of ladder, step back into ladder before moving forwards. Add ball – move through short ladder, collect ball and try to use similar small steps and good footwork at the same time as bouncing ball across a space. |
| **Expression (Game)** | (5 min) 4 marker spots placed in a 2-metre square. One team to each square. Each child in turn has 30 seconds to move around square and bounce the ball on each spot as often as possible. If a spot is missed the child must move to another corner. Keep a team score. |
| **Warm-down** | (5 min) Slow Dynamic FlexTM movements repeated, then static stretches. The advantage of the SAQ programme is that teachers and coaches can blend and fit a series of sessions into their own situations and produce quality movement experiences to suit the needs of the children under their care. Flexibility is the key, with the opportunity to match training with the experience and expertise of the teacher or coach. Further ideas for teachers based on QCA guidelines can be found in the appendix (p. 181) |

# Conclusion

It is hoped that your progress to this point in the book has filled you with inspiration and enjoyment. The use of the SAQ Junior Programme is both effective and extensive, covering all the abilities and aspirations found among children. As an enthusiastic and committed parent, teacher or coach you should now be armed with a whole new toolkit of activities and practices to build on the already good work that you are doing.

If the 'type' of child you are working with has not been catered for in this book, do not be disappointed as Sports-Specific SAQ Books exist for those children already specialising in developing their potential and special interests. Further publications dealing with a whole range of movement limiters, for example, dyspraxia, cerebral palsy and hemiplegia are planned and the table in the appendix (p. 159) gives an illustration of some of the basic activities already used in programmes with children requiring a more specific focus to their movement development.

| Y 6 | Perform skills at greater speed and develop control. Combine skills and mark a defender and space | Perform skills at greater speed |
|-----|-------------------------------------------------------------------------------------------------------|----------------------------------|

## KNOWLEDGE OF FITNESS AND HEALTH

### Key Stage 1

|  | Objectives | Outcomes |
|-----|-----------|----------|
| Y 1 | Being active is good for you and fun | Variety of running and evading<br>Practising movement skills can help a pupil feel warmer |
| Y 2 | What the body feels like during activity | Feel heart rate changing when playing different games |

### Key Stage 2

|  | Objectives | Outcomes |
|-----|-----------|----------|
| Y 3 | Describe the short-term effects of exercise | Describe how some games use short bursts of speed |

|  | Objectives | Outcomes |
|-----|-----------|----------|
| Y 4 | Recognise which activities help speed, strength and stamina<br>Know why stretching exercises increase range of movement and why this is important in games play | Make up suitable warm-up activities for games |

**Gymnastics** – Strength and suppleness priorities

|  | Objectives | Outcomes |
|---|---|---|
| **Y 5** | ■ Know and understand basic warm-up principles<br>■ Teach activities and exercises which will help most with speed, strength and stamina | ■ Choose ideas for warm-ups |

**Gymnastics** – Some static stretching e.g. shoulders and hamstrings

|  | Objectives | Outcomes |
|---|---|---|
| **Y 5** | ■ To understand the need to prepare properly for games | ■ How playing games can contribute to a healthy lifestyle |

|  | Outcomes | Objectives |
|---|---|---|
| **GYMNASTICS** | ■ Value of warming-up using stretching | ■ Explain how warming-up affects performance |
| **ATHLETICS** | ■ How athletics can increase strength, speed and stamina | ■ Know which types of exercise best help speed and flexibility development |

# SAQ JUNIOR PROGRAMME

In Year 3 Games children learn to outwit their opponents and score. They develop skills when finding and using space to keep the ball. They enter their opponents' territory with the ball and try to get into a good position for shooting (QCA Schemes of Work).

| SAMPLE LESSON PLAN USING APPROPRIATE OBJECTIVES AND OUTCOMES: Week 1. | |
|---|---|
| **AREA OF ACTIVITY** | **Games: Fundamental Movement** |
| **TOPIC** | **Introduction** |
| **Key Stage 1 – Y3 Invasion Games Touch Rugby** | |
| **LESSON AIM** | To develop understanding of how to score a try. |
| **LESSON OBJECTIVES** | AD  How to change speed and direction to get away from defender<br>SA  Use space, speed and direction changes to keep possession<br>KU  Warm-up activities helpful for invasion games<br>EV  Evaluate success of evading movements |
| **LESSON OUTCOMES** | ■ Perform attacking/dodging skills<br>■ To run with a rugby ball<br>■ Use a variety of tactics to keep ball<br>■ Exercises that help strength, speed and stamina<br>■ Explain why a performance is good |
| **Warm-up Dynamic Flex™** | (5 min) Use channel grid in fours. Perform jogs, skips, laterals, backwards, pre-turns, zigzag runs. |
| **Mechanics** | (5 min) Hurdles – Dead Leg, Leading Leg run and stride runs + burst off last hurdle to run and score a try. Repeat with teacher at front pointing to left/right. Children respond with a swerve on way to scoring. |
| **Movement and skill practice** | (10 min) Work in pairs – 1 v 1 'touch' game using evasive movement. |
| **Game** | (15 min) QCA Core Task 2. |
| **Warm-down** | Slow Dynamic Flex™ repeated, then static stretches. |

# Basic Movement Progressions

Work in fours – 3 v 1. Run and score a try at the other end of a 10 metre x 20 metre grid. The defender attempts to touch a runner with the ball. When touched the runner must stop and pass the ball to a team mate. Initially no passing other than this is allowed.

| Ladder work | |
|---|---|
| | ▪ Linear – Dead Leg moving right/left foot forwards in each square |
| | ▪ Linear – Dead Leg moving right/left foot sideways in each square |
| | ▪ Linear – Single step right foot lead, left foot steps beside, repeat |
| | ▪ Single step walk one foot in each square, alternate action |
| | ▪ Linear – Single step walk one foot in every second square to increase stride length |
| | ▪ Linear – Place hurdle at start and end of ladder and in the middle |
| | ▪ Linear – Place spots in different spaces to change step/stride pattern by stepping on or over |
| | ▪ Place spots on outsides of ladder to encourage a step 'out' onto spot |
| | ▪ Lateral – Single step right foot lead to right |
| | ▪ Single step left foot lead to left |
| | ▪ Repeat but after right/left step, step forwards out of ladder space with right or left foot before continuing, repeat in other direction (variation-step back instead of forwards) |
| | ▪ Place hurdle at start and end of ladder and in the middle to step over, moving sideways |
| | ▪ Combination Fold ladder into an L shape and repeat above with a change of direction |
| | ▪ Fold ladder in the other direction |
| **Spots** | |
| | ▪ 4 spots – standing; reach out with one foot to tap 1 of 3 spots in front |
| | ▪ Repeat placing spots to side or in a circle |
| | ▪ Use spots to determine step/stride patterns |
| | ▪ Use spots to determine standing lunge patterns – walking lunges |
| **Hurdles** | |
| | ▪ Dead Leg over 3 hurdles right foot/left foot lead |
| | ▪ Single step over hurdles (extend and vary spacing) |
| | ▪ A 'square gate' of hurdles to encourage stepping over in different directions |
| | ▪ 2 hurdles side by side and a spot on either side placed in the middle, step over hurdle on right step around spot and return over other hurdle in other direction, around other spot so moving in a circle. Repeat in other direction |

# Glossary

**Ability** — A stable, enduring, mainly genetically defined trait that underlies skilled performance

**Athleticism** — Having natural aptitude for physical activities

**Balance** — The ability to maintain equilibrium whilst in motion

**Bilateral exercise** — Using both arms or legs at the same time to perform an exercise

**Biomechanics** — The science that examines the internal and external factors acting on a human body and the effects produced by these forces

**Complex movements** — The movements of many body parts as well as the co-ordination among them in time

**Concentric muscle contraction** — Contraction that involves shortening of the contracted muscle

**Co-ordination** — The ability to perform accurate tasks often involving the use of the senses and a series of correlated muscular contractions affecting a range of joints and therefore relative limb and body positions

**Eccentric muscle contraction** — Contraction that involves lengthening of the contracted muscle

**Fire/firing** — The fast activation of

**muscles** — specific muscle groups

**Fitness** — The ability to carry out tasks without undue fatigue

**Flexibility** — The range of motion through which the limbs or body parts are permitted to move

**Functional movements** — Movements which have a specific purpose i.e. those which relate to the specific requirements of an activity

**Health** — Of strong constitution, producing well-being and vigour

**Innervate** — To stimulate, to transmit a nervous energy to a muscle

**Mechanics** — The technical aspects of movement

**Motor skills** — Skills where the primary determinant of success are the movement components themselves

**Neuro-muscular system** — The link between the Central Nervous System and Muscular System

**Plyometrics** — Drills or exercises linking sheer strength and scope of movement to produce an explosive-reactive type of movement

**Programmed-learning** — The acquisition of new patterns of action

**Proprioception** — Sensory information arising from the body, resulting in the sense of position and movement

**Reps** — The number of times a task, such as a work interval or lifting of a weight, is repeated

**Rhythm** — A sequence of regularly recurring functions

**Set** — A group of repetitions

**Simple movements** — A movement involving a small number of joint motions and where co-ordination among limbs is minimised

**Skill** — A capability to bring about an end result with maximum certainty, minimum energy, or minimum time

**Strategies** — Overall plans for success

**Strength** — The force that a muscle or muscle group can exert against a resistance

**Tactics** — Detailed patterns of movement

**Timing** — The process of regulating an action to produce the best effect

**Training** — An exercise programme to develop an athlete for a particular event. Increasing skill of performance and energy capacities are of equal consideration

**Velocity** — Speed or rate of movement

# Bibliography and references

Pearson, A. E. *SAQ Rugby* (2001). A&C Black, London.

Pearson, A. E. *SAQ Soccer* (2001). A&C Black, London.

Pearson, A. E. *SAQ Women's Soccer* (2003). A&C Black, London.

Pearson, A. E. and Naylor, S. *SAQ Hockey* (2003). A&C Black, London.

Pearson, A. E. *Dynamic Flexibility* (2004). A&C Black, London.

Pearson, A. E. *Fit 4 Work* (2003). A&C Black, London.

Bailey, Richard and Macfadyen, Tony (2000). *Teaching Physical Education 5-11*, pp. 77–80. Continuum, London.

Bennett, S. (1999). t-and-f: New muscle research findings. *Muscle Symposium*. AIS, Canberra, Australia.

Buroker, K. C. and Schwane, J. A. (1989). Does post exercise stretching alleviate DOMS. *Physician and Sportsmedicine*, 17/6: 65–83.

De Vries, H. (1986). *Physiology of Exercise – For Physical Education and Athletics*, pp. 462–72, 474–87,482–8. Wm. C. Brown, Dubuque, Iowa, USA.

Enoka R.M. (1994). *Neuromechanical Basis of Kinesiology.* Human Kinetics:USA.

Fowles, J. R., Sale, D. G. and MacDougall, J. D. (2000). Reduced strength after passive stretch of the human plantarflexors. *Journal of Applied Physiology*, 89: 1179–88.

Gallahue, David L. and Cleland Donnelly, Frances (2003). *Developmental Physical Education for all Children*, p. 54. Human Kinetics, USA.

Gleim, G.W. and McHugh, M. P. (1997). Flexibility and its effects on sports injury and performance. *Sports Medicine* 24/5: 289–99.

Herbert, R. D. and Gabriel, M. G. (2002). Effects of stretching before and after exercising on muscle soreness and risk of injury: A systematic review. *British Medical Journal*, 325: 468.

Morley, D. and Bailey, R. (2003). Using Dynamic Assessment to Identify Potential Talent in Physical Education – Incorporating an SAQ Programme.

Moscov, J. G. (1993). *Static ROM, Leg Power and Strength as Predictors of Dynamic ROM in Female Ballet Dancers.* Microform Publications, University of Oregon, Eugene, Oregon.

Nicolson, R. I. and Fawcett, A. J. (1990). *Automaticity: A New Framework for Dyslexia Research.* Cognition, 35(2) 159–182.

Pope, R. P., Herbert, R. D. and Kirwan, J. D. (2000). A randomised trial of pre-exercise stretching for the prevention of lower limb injury. *Medicine and Science in Sports and Exercise*, 32: 271–7.

Portwood, Madeleine (2003). *Dyslexia and Physical Education*, pp. 7–9. David Fulton, London.

Portwood, Madeleine (2000). *Developmental Dyspraxia, Identification and Intervention A Manual for Parents and Professionals.* David Fulton, London.

Qualifications and Curriculum Authority (QCA) *Physical Education Schemes of Work* – www.qca.org.uk.

Rosenbaum, D. and Hennig, E. M. (1995). The influence of stretching and warm up exercises on Achilles tendon reflex activity. *Journal of Sports Sciences*, 13: 481–90.

Schilling, B. K. and Stone, M. H. (2000). Stretching: acute effects on strength and performance. *Strength and Conditioning Journal*, 22/1: 44–7.

Shrier, I. (1999). Stretching before exercise does not reduce the risk of local muscle injury: a critical review of the clinical and basic science literature. *Clinical Journal of Sports Medicine*, 9: 221–7.

Smith, L. L., Brunetz, M. H., Cheiner, T. C., McCammon, M. R., Houmard, J. A., Franklin, M. E. and Israel, R. G. (1993). The effects of static and ballistic stretching on DOMS and Creatin Kinase. *Research Quarterley for Exercise and Sport*; 64/1: 103–7.

# Index of drills